For the Love of Community

Life Lessons From A Small Town

Written,

Edited and Compiled by

Dr. Roland Tolliver

and

Dr. Stephen Spyrison

Celebrate your Community!
Roland Tolliver

enJoy!
Steve Spyrison

Kastle Publishing   Freeport, Illinois 61032

Kastle Publishing

A Freeport, Lincoln-Douglas Kiwanis Project

Mark Victor Hansen
Author and Editor, #1 New York Times bestselling series Chicken Soup for the Soul®
Feel really inspired at the soul level and read this great gift of inspiration and wisdom. Read it, enjoy it, and pass it along to someone you love!

Alan Wenzel
Executive Director, Leadership Institute
Highland Community College
Dr. Roland Tolliver and Dr. Stephen Spyrison have given yet another gift to the residents of Northwest Illinois. Created under their caring guidance and leadership, **For the Love of Community** is filled with stories which will lift your spirit and touch your heart. The examples of love, caring and community involvement you will read here may not be unique to our corner of the world, but certainly define who we are as a people.

Olga Gize Carlile, assistant managing editor of *The Journal-Standard*, who writes a daily column, "Around the Table."
There are diamonds to be mined in our own backyard. And that's exactly what Dr. Roland Tolliver and Dr. Stephen Spyrison did in their book, **For the Love of Community**. Always impressed by the stories they heard from friends and associates -- not the headline stories -- but everyday stories from the heart -- they gathered these. In their first book, **For the Love of Community**, they preserved these for all of us to share. As a journalist, I have always said, "There is a story in everyone" and found it so "Around the Table" and so have Dr. Tolliver and Dr. Spyrison. This book will be read with joyful enthusiasm. They have found the "diamonds," and the community will celebrate.

Dottie Walters, Author, *Speak & Grow Rich*, Prentice Hall,
President, Walters International Speakers' Bureau,
Publisher, *Sharing Ideas* Newsmagazine
If ever there was a book which inspires us all not to go to our grave with a song unsung, it is **For the Love of Community**. These stories of inspiration, courage and purpose are like vitamins for the heart. Well done, Dr. Roland Tolliver and Dr. Stephen Spyrison. Splendid!

Jeff Rogers, managing Editor, *The Journal-Standard*
There are no stories more important than those that reflect the good in a community. The people of northwest Illinois are good, caring and sharing people and it is heartwarming to see this collaborative effort to bring their stories together. Enjoy.

Glenna R. Salsbury, CSP, CPAE
Author of *The Art of a Fresh Start*,
(1997-1998 President of the National Speakers Association,)
"This is a book destined to open your heart and mind to the incredible community of people in which you dwell. Don't miss it!!!"

Love: The One Creative Force

Spread love everywhere you go: first of all in your own house. Give love to your children, to your wife or husband, to a next door neighbor...Let no one ever come to you without leaving better and happier. Be the living expression of God's kindness: kindness in your face, kindness in your eyes, kindness in your smile, kindness in your warm greeting.

Mother Teresa

Dedication

We dedicate this book with love to our wives, Irena and Vicki, and to our children, Mary, Veronica, Claire, and Teresa, and Sarah, Ben and Tyler. God has truly blessed us with your love.

We also dedicate this book to all the people of our community of Northwest Illinois. You are an inspiration to us and we are honored to live here.

This printing is in memory of Merl Blackwood, whose art graces the front cover of the book, and to Ruth Hiatt, whose story was told by her niece, Colleen, in *My Aunt Ruth*. Both of these fine people died in 1998. May their memories, talents and good works be an inspiration to us all.

Contents

3. Joys of Parenting

4. Quiet Heroes

5. Overcoming Adversity

6. Creativity in the Community

7. Community History and Community Spirit

Acknowledgments

For the Love of Community has taken us close to 18 months to go from concept to reality. It has truly been a labor of love to write, edit and compile the stories that are a part of this book. It could not have been accomplished without the contributions of numerous people who made it all possible.

Our families- Irena, Mary, Veronica, Claire, and Teresa Tolliver and Vicki, Sarah, Ben, and Tyler Spyrison, without your love, support, and understanding none of this could have happened.

Our parents- My father, Roland, Sr. and his wife , Dreama, for whom I keep in my thoughts daily; and in memory of my mother, Mary, to whom I am indebted for my sense of adventure and creativity; and to my mother, Betty Mae and to my father, Harry and his wife, Mary, for their love and support and to whom I have never expressed enough appreciation and thanks.

Our staffs- Nancy Charlie, Erin, Jessie and Sandi, and especially Dr. Doug Mason, who took over on many occasions while I was working on the book or learning about the book world. Joan, Linda, Walter, Barb, Brenda, Alicia, and Allison who fielded the calls and handled the mail for my *other job.*

John Cook, Julia Mills-Ruckman and Joan Walsh for their editing expertise.

Merl Blackwood, Duane Smith, and the late Kenneth Fissell for their art work; Kurt Koester, Steve Snyder and Sarah Giaimo for photography; their contributions to the book are invaluable.

Taylor, Tanya, Marsha, Betty, Jan, Ron, and Bev our mastermind partners, who gave us the creative encouragement we often needed.

The Lincoln-Douglas Kiwanis Club for their commitment to another one of *our* projects.

The Journal Standard, the Freeport Arts Center, Book World, Eastrich Printing, Wendy Gustafson and the marketing department at Freeport Memorial Hospital, and WFRL for their assistance in publicizing the book and the requests for stories.

Mark Victor Hansen, Jack Canfield and Dottie Walters, consummate professionals, who offered their guidance to these fledgling authors; and the hundreds of authors of the *Chicken Soup* series, whose stories continually inspired us.

A very special thank you to Mark Wagner and Wagner Printing for their cooperation, assistance and efforts in printing our first book.

A heartfelt thanks to everyone who either wrote or contributed a story or poem. Your time, energy and talent are the soul of the book. While all the submissions were greatly appreciated, we regret that not all of your stories could be published. We commend each of you for the effort you put forth and the love that went into each of the stories and poems.

We realize that there are many more people that have contributed in one way or another to *For the Love of Community: Northwest Illinois.* To each of you we say, "Thank you." To all of the people of Northwest Illinois, this is your community. Remember that we all really do need one another and that we are all of one community. Keep working together and good things are bound to happen.

We are grateful for what our community gives to us and this is our humble offering to the community we love. Above all else, we want to keep in mind that, "with God all things are possible."

Introduction

In November, 1995 I wrote in my journal, "Every person has a story to tell." The phrase had been floating around in my mind with no apparent direction. What was I to do with it? Several months later I read a book that gave me the direction I was looking for. *Chicken Soup for the Soul* was not just a collection of short stories, but a quilt in written form. One that took the cold out of a winter night. One that was weaved together in a fashion that described the essence of our beings. One that eventually brought back the phrase from the popular bumper sticker, "Think Globally. Act Locally." I had the opportunity to meet Mark Victor Hansen for the first time in October, 1996 and presented him with my idea of the book, tentatively titled (presumptuously, I might add) *Chicken Soup for the Community Soul.* I forgot about a little item called a copyright. With a test market of twenty friends our new working title became, *For the Love of Community.* I had enlisted Dr. Steve Spyrison, my best friend and initial mastermind partner to collaborate with me on the project. We were in the middle of the Highland Community College Leadership Institute course at the time and figured, "How much work could it be?" Obviously, a lot more than we anticipated! Our initial publicity for stories was a simple flyer that we passed out at local literary events, the book store, library, and community centers. An article and follow-up editorial helped us on our way. Eventually, more than one hundred stories were sent in, dropped off, or contributed in some way.

We feel that these stories will touch your hearts, teach a few lessons, bring tears of joy, laughter, and even in several instances inform you about your community and the people that are your neighbors. The art of storytelling has been losing out to the fast-paced action of our society. History of family, history of community, and history of the world have all been passed down through the years by means of storytelling. If we can encourage one family to sit down and enlighten their children about their heritage, their hopes and dreams, and their love, this book will be worth every second spent on it.

We have carefully chosen three charities from which the proceeds of this book will be donated. The first is the **Head Start** program of Northwest Illinois. Our Lincoln-Douglas Kiwanis club donates our money, time, and talents to helping these children each year. We have read to them, helped build their buildings, hosted them for a Thanksgiving dinner and purchased books for the children and their families. Our primary objective is to see that each child has a chance to learn to read, do well in school, and contribute to society.

Our second charity is for **Adult Literacy** in Northwest Illinois. These programs are coordinated through Highland Community College. Stephenson County alone has over 20 percent illiteracy among our adult population. Many people cannot venture beyond their neighborhoods or communities because they cannot read directions or street signs. There are many wonderful volunteers who donate their time to these programs. They need your assistance in spreading the good news that help is available for the asking. We believe that an educated, well-informed society can only benefit all of us.

The third charity is the **United Leukodystrophy Foundation**. This is a voluntary organization consisting of parents, physicians, researchers and private individuals who aid those with a life threatening, degenerative neurological disorder. It is not well-known and receives very little government assistance for research and treatment. There are many different types of this hereditary condition that primarily affects young children, most of whom fail to live past the first or second decade of life. As I tried to depict in the story, "God's Gift", my daughter, Claire has been diagnosed with leukodystrophy. The Foundation and its members have been a source of inspiration during these trying times. It is grossly under funded and can use our help. We felt that it is important to give back something to those who have given of themselves so willingly.

If you would have a desire to contribute to any one of these organizations, please contact one of us and we can pass on the information you would need.

We hope that in some small way we can contribute to the community through this endeavor. If you enjoy the book, share it with a friend or family member. Send one to a relative who has moved away and remind them of the great things and people of our communities in Northwest Illinois. We look forward to hearing from you after you have read the book. Our wish is that it will spark a memory or inspire you to share a story with a loved one. If you want, you may even share a story with us for a future edition.

So turn off the television, let the answering machine get the phone, pull up your favorite blanket, get a cup of tea, and enjoy what each story, poem, and memory has to offer. You deserve it!

Dr. Roland Tolliver
Dr. Stephen Spyrison

Authors' Notes

Dear Al,

I would like to express a special thanks to you. You have not only been the driving force behind this book, but you have been my closest friend, a mentor and a spiritual guide, as well. No words can adequately express my appreciation.

Steve

Dear Steve,

I am forever indebted to you for your willingness to participate in the development of this book. Your constant encouragement saw me through many trying days. It has been a pleasure to write, edit and compile this book with you. Most of all, Steve, thank you for your friendship.

Al

1

Tributes

We cannot hold a torch to light another's path without brightening our own.

Ben Sweetland

Kenneth Fissell

New Year

A TIME FOR REMEMBERING, LETTING GO

New beginnings, old endings. Things change. Babies are born, people die... and people have to go on.

As many of you know, I took a three-month leave of absence during my husband Frank's courageous battle with cancer.

It was the hardest thing I ever had to go through, and in the end I lost my soul mate, and the animals of Stephenson County lost a man who quietly worked behind the scenes to make life better for them.

I first met Frank when an ad appeared in the paper asking anyone interested in the welfare of the dogs and cats in Stephenson County to please come to a meeting at the library. He claimed that as I walked into the room he said to himself, "There's the girl I plan to marry!"

Frank was vice president of the humane society and we were thrown together since I was the new manager.

Frank was always repairing painting or building something for the animals, and when we opened our first shelter, it was in the basement of a house on Walnut Street.

Frank worked hard getting the place ready. What fun we all had, that small group of dedicated people, working to get the doors open, and open we did!

We soon found the building on Monterey Street and then the work really began. That group of determined people burned the candle many a night after their own full day at work.

Under Frank's quiet direction we soon turned the building into a workable shelter. We were all tireless and relentless in trying to do it all, and in two short months we opened our doors to the public.

Again Frank continued in the background. He always seemed to have a hammer or saw in his hands. Something always needed to be fixed or built.

The night he and I brought the bathtub home in his truck, we almost lost it at a busy intersection. Then we stayed up half the night hooking it up so the dogs could get a bath the next day. That was the night he proposed to me and I knew that I could not let this gentle man slip out of my life.

By then Frank was the president of the humane society, and so he had to voluntarily resign from the board since I was the manager.

Everyone called it "puppy love." Many wondered if it would last. But most knew that, whether in an official capacity or a volunteer behind the scenes, his only concern was for all the animals in Stephenson County.

Every time the police called us at night for an animal run, he was dressed and had the truck started before I had hung up the phone. And it wasn't that he wouldn't say no to helping the animals, he couldn't say no.

In a world where recognition and popularity and praise seem to be sought after, Frank seemed to hang back in the shadows, quietly but steadily working, building, painting or cleaning pens.

Frank's mom must have had quite an insight into the man Frank would become, because she named him after the saint for the animals, St. Francis of Assisi. His middle name was Joseph, after that quiet carpenter of long ago who also was working behind the scenes.

So appropriately, I end this year in extreme sadness and begin the New Year by taking up my pen and continuing on alone. I lost my soul mate, my better half, and the animals lost a gentle being who cared for life itself.

I know he would be telling me; "Don't stop...Don't give up...Don't quit caring. The pets of Stephenson County need people like you, June." But, the good Lord knew – it was a man like Frank they needed.

Sometimes we are touched by a friend
Who never asks for much,
But quietly goes about his work
Giving it just the right touch.
Who knew how long he'd be here?
Who thought to say we care;
Who remembered to tell him thank you?
His presence was a blessing so very dear
That now in his absence he is still here.

June Krogull

To live as fully, as completely as possible, to be happy...is the true aim and end to life.

Llewellyn Powers

DOUG VEDRA

The phone rang at 6:30 a.m. on December 21, 1996. As I reached for the phone, I thought to myself, " who didn't come into work today?", because as a Director of Nursing I have the wonderful opportunity to produce staff out of nowhere. When I am not successful, I have the privilege of going to work myself. I normally don't mind, but today I was exhausted. The past two weeks had been both physically and emotionally draining, not only for myself, but the entire family.

I answered the phone. It was my younger brother Bill. He said that mom needed to talk to me. Mom came to the phone, and before the words came through the tears, I knew it was the phone call I had been dreading. She told me that Doug had died a little after 6 a.m., and that she would talk to me later in the morning. It was the morning of Doug's birthday, he turned 43. My heart felt as though it had fallen into my stomach, and I started to sob.

My big brother had died, the person who had taught me so much, who got me my first job, who taught me how to fish, the guy who helped me overcome my fear of heights by making me climb up the waterfall steps at Krape Park, by standing right behind me on the same step so I would not fall. This person was gone from my life.

Doug was diagnosed with cancer in late August, 1996, and from the time he became ill, his prognosis had been poor. The cancer had spread from his lungs into his liver and his bones by the time he was diagnosed.

Doug never gave in to the disease, and he never let anyone else give up. Doug laid some strict ground rules for his family, and because of their love and commitment, Louanne and the four children did all they could to allow Doug to live his final days at home, with each of them at his side.

Louanne took the family leave act, and literally never left Doug's side. Doug II moved home from college to help care for his dad. Emily, Dan, and Erika all took turns staying with their dad. When Doug would request pineapple upside down cake at 11 p.m., off to the kitchen Emily and Dan went to attempt to meet their dad's request, only to find out the task was a little more than they had bargained for.

Many people believe that angels do not come to earth in human form, but Doug and his family are living proof that angels do come in all shapes and sizes.

Doug walked each of us through his dying process, in the hopes that our roads would be less lonely when he was no longer with us physically. At the time, I could not see the great dignity and strength with which he was approaching his death and the profound courage Louanne and the children had to allow and encourage Doug to die with the same pride, dignity, and determination with which he lived his life.

Doug contributed his time and talents to the community, along with his family, and when Doug needed his community, they were there, in astounding numbers to show their love and support with cards, gifts, cash donations, food and constant encouragement and, most importantly, prayers.

We buried Doug on a cold and snowy day, and while Doug is not with us in person, we are surrounded by his love and laughter with which he lived his short but accomplished life.

We all love you Doug and miss you greatly!!!

Susan Vedra-Fulton

Whom God loves dies young.

Meander

Candi and K.C.

From the day the doctors told me something terrible was wrong with my children, a part of me died. The hopes and dreams that every mother holds for her children had vanished. The sleepovers with friends, the football games, prom, planning the wedding, seeing my grandchildren born were no longer a reality. Without a name for the illness that would someday take their lives, I felt hopeless. I grasped at straws, only to receive many unfulfilled promises by "professionals" who had a cure for everything.

One day I realized how precious the time left really was. They said adulthood — 18? 21? Only God knew for sure. I realized I must focus on the positive and give these children a whole life of living in a very short time. Everywhere we traveled, people would stare, ask questions or make comments. Later we would joke about some of the comments and how THEY were the truly "unusual" ones.

They were just as normal as any other children or young adults. They were both very intelligent and caring — never selfish. Their smiles were worth a million dollars, and their laugh, almost identical to one another, were truly unique.

Candi, like most women, loved to shop. She picked out her own prom dress — after shopping seven different stores, moving racks of clothing from side to side to make room for her large, reclining wheelchair — only to return to the first dress and the first store we shopped. Just like a woman.

Tributes

K.C., like most men, loved his sports. Football and basketball were his favorites. Not too many games went by without him making a friendly wager with a friend. Always taking the underdog was his style, and there wasn't a sport's statistic he didn't know.

You could read their eyes and facial expressions. You knew when they wanted a drink, their word boards to communicate, or later, when they were in pain.

Candi was a very brave girl. She was at peace with herself, God, and the world. She and K.C. had an inseparable bond. It's almost as though she were showing him the way. I still see her smile.

These children have touched so many lives. One would wonder how someone so severely physically challenged could be so happy. But, they had a lust for life. They had extreme gratitude for the simple things in life. They turned lemons into lemonade. They taught me patience. People would say they didn't know how lucky they were because their children were not "handicapped." Instead, they don't know how lucky we were to have each other. Thank you, God, for Candi and K.C.

Candi Denton: November 27, 1974 - November 7, 1992
K.C. Denton: December 16, 1978 -August 5, 1997

Linda Rae

The Road Home

(In loving memory of Dale and Guy Brinkmeier)

"Are we there yet?" a voice calls out from the back seat of the van, and I have to giggle as my husband answers that question for the third time.

We live in Pearl City and we're driving home from Freeport, which is only ten miles away, after visiting their grandparents. I can recall having asked my parents the same question a time or two. In fact, it seems like it was just yesterday they were taking this same drive with me and my sisters to visit our grandparents. They lived in a house that's just two miles from where we live now.

So many beautiful memories were created in that little old school house my grandparents lived in. The second you walked through the door, you were embraced by warmth, love and kindness. My grandparents loved each other very much. Their love was so strong that not only did it live in their hearts and ours, but it must have lived in the walls too, because no matter how many (or how few) people there were in that little five room house, that love was always strong and never ending.

We had such fun there. My sisters and I helped in the yard, with cookouts and picking up horseshoes for grandpa and our dad. We spent a lot of time playing hide-n-seek, status, tag, baseball and horseshoes. Christmastime was always a special time for our family. We also gathered for Easter and the Fourth of July. Memorial Day was when we had our first summer cookout, which always symbolized the beginning of summer to me when I was a little girl.

Grandma always made us delicious baked goods to have for a snack. I remember also that grandma loved to fly kites, and not just any kite, but her beautiful dragon kite. It was such a big kite! We would run around in an empty corn field and she would make the kite dive down at us. Then, just when we would squeal

9

and duck, she would make it go back up into the sky. Sometimes she would help us to fly the dragon, which was a special treat, but never as fun as running and having her catch us and watching her face light up when we would yell.

Grandpa loved to play horseshoes and Atari. He would play games with us on his Atari, and I think he let us win a time or two. Laughter from grandpa was a regular thing. I always loved his laugh. It made me feel that all was right with the world. He got a lot of joy out of the different kinds of wind up toys there were. I remember him showing us a spider he had, and he laughed joyously every time he wound it up. One year grandpa made all of his grandchildren, (5 at the time) latch hook pictures. I still have mine. It is a picture of Cookie Monster. It has seen better days, but it is one of my most treasured gifts.

I was afraid it would be too painful to live so close to where some of my happiest and most cherished childhood memories were created. It has been just the opposite though. I am so thankful for having moved to Pearl City. It has helped me to heal.

The time I spent at my grandparents' surrounded by that love-the special love of family-is what helped make me the person that I am today. I can only hope to surround my own children with the same feeling of love, warmth and security.

As we pull into the driveway, one of the boys calls out, "We're home!"

With a warm heart, I smile. "Yes, we are home." I look to the sky knowing that my grandparents are watching over us and our home with love.

Sherri Bunn

Example is not the main thing in influencing others. It is the only thing.

Albert Schweitzer

A Tribute to Judy Keith

Dear Judy,

Today, for a few moments, we are writing this letter to express our personal thoughts to you. It has been almost three years now since you passed away and went to your heavenly home. The gates of time open up so quickly. It seems like only yesterday that you left us, and yet it seems like an eternity.

We remember how we became acquainted with you. We met you as a secretary in the Attendance/Business office at the Freeport Junior High School. We became close friends as we worked together. Your beautiful smile was contagious, and the warmth in your voice reflected your kindness as you welcomed the world into your office.

It was easy to recognize your deep concern for others and your loyalty to all with whom you came in contact. Your patience during difficult circumstances was a trait we wanted to emulate. In spite of a demanding and busy work schedule, you took time to make each person — from staff members to parents to students — feel so welcome in your office. You provided extra guidance to parents with such compassion, especially to the needy who were apprehensive about handling school business matters. You honored the difficult to love. Truly, you saw Christ in everyone.

Students were drawn to you because you were there for them, and you cared about their individual needs. So many who came to your office had no one to listen to them or to support them, but you made each one feel so important. Neither race, nor color, nor religion mattered to you. You loved them all from the depths of your heart like a caring mother.

Do you remember how many coats you bought for those girls who didn't have warm clothing for winter? You were dedicated to helping others in need, putting them first in your life. One of the students whom you befriended attended your funeral service and personally mentioned that she wouldn't have been there if it hadn't been for your support during a crucial time in her life. What a lasting tribute to your life and the giving of yourself!

When you had to leave your job at school to battle cancer, no one ever forgot you. We prayed daily for your recovery and your return. Even during those difficult days and months, you were optimistic and caring. Pain did not discourage you as you faced each day courageously. You were always thankful to God for His tender care and for your devoted husband, Gary, and for your loving family who encouraged and cared for you. You thanked God for your friends and for your prayer warriors.

As we close this letter, we thank you, Judy, for being our special friend. Even though you were never able to return to us, we know you are dwelling in Heaven today looking out for us. All of your earthly suffering has ceased. And we will join you someday. What a blessed hope!

Your precious life will always be in our memories. The following words taken from *Kindness, Heartland Messengers*, aptly describe your personal philosophy of life:

I shall pass this way but once;
Any good therefore, that I can do or
Any kindness that I can show to
Any human being, let me do it now.
Let me not defer or neglect it, for
I shall not pass this way again.

Love,
    Your friends,
    Joyce Spahn
    Judy Pettit

My Big Sister Jane

She left Oklahoma, the prairie state of her birth, in the early 20's to come to the dangerous city of Chicago to find a job and enter the Art Institute to study interior design.

What a big dream for an inexperienced young lady with very little money but lots of ambition. Choosing a career over marriage was not the popular thing to do at that time.

This was my sister Jane, twelve years my senior, who always looked after me all the days of her life.

I remember the day I started school. There were five of us in our family entering the same school. I couldn't find my way to my classroom and it was Jane who found me and quickly took me to where I belonged.

This must have been humiliating for a teenager to have to care for a crying little sister. She reported to my mother that I stood in a corner crying. I insisted, "I might have been sweatin' but I wasn't cryin,"— the first lie I ever told.

She and I shared a bedroom and became very good friends as we both grew.

After a year and a half in the local college, she taught school for a year in a tiny town nearby. I went to visit her. She took me out for a soda one evening. I accidentally pulled the soda glass to the edge of the table and the bottom part fell to the floor and broke. This time I really cried from embarrassment and humiliation. But Jane, in her lady-like way comforted me and reassured me, trying to build my self esteem.

Later she took a job in our home town. One day, dressed as the tom-boy that I was (growing up in the midst of four brothers) I drifted into her place of business. I wanted to tell her about a beautiful bathing suit I had seen in a shop window. She gave me a lecture on my appearance and told me never to come back dressed as I was. I was crushed, until she came home that evening bringing me that beautiful bathing suit I had admired so greatly.

After my first year at college, the Great Depression was at its depth. Finances were strained in our big family. I decided to find a job in Oklahoma City. Stopping to visit a friend on the way to the city, I had a phone call from my mother.

Jane had written a savage letter urging me to stay in college. I made a U-turn. When I reached home there was a big bag of goodies from Jane, including a new coat and three new dresses from Carson, Pirie, Scott and Co. That label made me feel very well dressed on the plains of Oklahoma. Jane had gotten a job at Carson's and was studying at the Art Institute.

When she was employed as a decorator/consultant at the F. A. Read Co. in Freeport, she had a wild idea that I should move from Oklahoma to Freeport to teach. To my great surprise I was accepted.

So thanks to Jane, I not only found a nice teaching job in a nice town, but, not long afterward, found a nice Freeport man to be my husband.

Jane and I had about three years together in Freeport before she decided to go back to Chicago. Eventually she opened her own shop on North Michigan Avenue.

Jane was always a loving and giving person, not just to family but to many others. When World War II came along, she enlisted in the American Red Cross. She was sent to Europe and her assignment was to travel with the forward troops to convert conquered villas and other buildings into rest and recreation centers for the troops. When the war ended she came to us for a much needed rest and finally went back to her own shop in Chicago.

She enjoyed our children and had them visit her often. They loved to go, but always complained about having to wear their Sunday clothes every day.

When we had a good snow, the Freeport Country Club opened its hills to the town children. I remember Jane, even in her fifties, sliding down the hills with our children on their toboggan. Jane taught me to love beauty in all aspects—generosity, caring and sharing home and family.

One might say, "How wonderful to have a sister like that!" I say, "How wonderful to BE a sister like that."

Virginia Babock

Aunt Mary

When I was growing up, relatives were people you could count on. Oh–I knew from reading stories that there were untrustworthy bounders out there. But they weren't my relatives. Relatives were people you could count on.

And my Aunt Mary was a prime example. She was a proverbial Rock of Gibraltar. My mother was one of the youngest in a large family. Mary was one of the oldest and was the wise advisor. She had had an illustrious career in nursing and, rather late in life, married one of her patients. Aunt Mary ran her house and her husband the way she had directed her hospital ward. She knew the right way to do things–and they were done that way.

She was a plump, rather severe looking older woman when I knew her best. She was, in fact, old enough to be my grandmother. But she had a warm heart under that organized and fussy exterior. She and Uncle Leroy had no children, so they took a special interest in all of Mary's nieces and nephews. Proper and quiet behavior was always insisted upon. When we visited them in Erie, Pennsylvania, it would never have occurred to us to wander far from Aunt Mary's straight and narrow path.

Although she and Uncle Leroy had extremely modest means, they could be very generous with us when the need arose. Not only were we urged to go on to college–we received loans to help us continue.

I remember Aunt Mary best from the first years of the Great Depression, the early 1930's. In those difficult times money was very scarce. Aunt Mary was extremely frugal and she was in complete charge of the purse strings. I still laugh when I think of one example of her penny pinching. She belonged for many years to a group of eight women who met weekly for dessert and program. When she died my uncle gave me, in memory of her, their set of sterling silver flatware. And Uncle Leroy carefully explained that, while it was a set for eight, I would find only seven dessert forks. This was because one of the eight women in Aunt Mary's group never ate dessert–so she had only needed to buy seven forks.

Another example of Aunt Mary's frugality makes me feel rueful when I remember it. One year she and Uncle Leroy drove from northern Pennsylvania to Virginia, where I was a lonely and homesick eleven-year-old in boarding schools. They came to take me to Washington, D.C., as a weekend treat. It was spring. The cherry blossoms were in bloom. The sun shone. And my aunt and uncle did all they could to make it a memorable time for me. It was memorable, too–but I am ashamed to say that what I remember most was the fact that they had found a room in a Tourist Home (that's Tourist Home with a capital T and a capital H–in those days motels were unknown). We spent two nights there–and my aunt saw no reason why she should pay extra for a cot for me. I had to sleep between them in the double bed.

I recall many holidays when they opened their home to me–for I was going to school on the East Coast, and it cost too much to consider taking the train all the way back to the Middle West for short vacations. So for Christmas and Easter I usually visited them–and they always seemed so glad to see me. But the visit I recall most vividly is one they made to us. We lived in northern Indiana at the edge of a town–really out in the country, with fields stretching off for miles to the south of us. The prairie grass was high that summer–and dry from weeks of no rain. We saw smoke in the distance one noon. Aunt Mary insisted on eating her lunch upstairs in the bathroom, from which she could watch the progress of the fire. In the early afternoon the wind shifted, and a wall of flame rushed towards us. Aunt Mary must have made her plans when she was monitoring things at lunchtime. While my mother was using the hose to wet the house and garage walls and while we three children were ready with brooms and shovels to beat out flames, my uncle got ready to move their car and my aunt disappeared into the house. When I ran in the front door a few moments later she was just coming out, her arms full of their possessions, to put in their car. "I'm coming right back for your family's things she told me as she rushed by. But then she stopped a moment to ask why I was coming in. I told her a man dressed only in his bathing trunks had been rowing on the river–had seen the fire–and had come to see if he could help. But he needed shoes. "Here," she said, "take your uncle's Sunday shoes." And she handed them to me on the spot. Our house survived–with only a scorched wall on the garage. But I think my little brother still feels a bit of a grudge. Aunt Mary made him sit out of harm's way, guarding their car and its contents, across the street by the river, while everyone else got to share in the excitement of battling the flames.

You can see why I remember my Aunt Mary.

Lois Harlan (copyright)

16

June

My sister, June
Was seventeen months older,
and, she should have taken
Care of me. O how different I might be
If she wasn't born a cretin.
Kids knew she wasn't quite right,
And kids did, as kids do,
Be mean, make her a fool, so,
I fought her battles too.
I am kind.
I am compassionate,
I am strong and humane,
All because of June.

Milda Morse

Minnie B., My Grandmother

What was she really-like—this handsome, stubborn woman of English descent from Mineral Point, Wisconsin—who helped her husband found a world-wide pharmaceutical company right here in Pretzelville? Minnie Belle was her whole name; woe to those who called her "Minnie." Friends and family shortened it to "Minnie B." This was okay—kind of sporty. Gramie liked sporty things...long black Packards, Buffalo Bill's Wild West Show and sulky racing at Taylor Park.

She married W.T. Rawleigh at 17 and they immediately moved to Freeport. Grampa was just 20 and already 'on the road' with his health products. First they made them in their home; by 1895 they'd organized their first corporation. Meanwhile, Grandmother had become a visiting nurse and borne two children. She'd also become a church pillar and a fabulous cook.

I recall the annual bake sales at Embury Methodist Church. Men actually had fist fights over Minnie B.'s cakes and pies. Nobody could touch her baked beans; her ham loaf was fit for gods. After dinner at Gramie's house I always took a nap. Her English Spaghetti and Cornish Pie recipes are still family secrets. At church picnics people always asked, "At which table is Minnie B.?"

She always spoke straight-forwardly; never minced words, Her gift for nursing was God-given. She went from home to home helping all—with a special feeling for children. Maybe this was because World War I took her only son. She helped found the King's Daughters Orphanage and donated land for its expansion.

Often she quoted the Bible. Cleanliness was truly next to Godliness in Minnie B's book. On occasion she scrubbed the public sidewalk in front of her house. On her hands and knees.

As I pass her house now, still standing much the same on Stephenson Street, I can see her clearly. Sitting on her couch, wearing an apron, hands folded...looking pensive and a mite wistful in the eventide. She would be very quiet. When I'd ask what she was doing, she'd smile and say, "Counting my blessings, child, counting my blessings."

Anna Belle K. Nimmo

Thomas Pfisterer
(1894-1996)

*The remembrance of the good done by those we love
is the only consolation left when we have lost them.*

Demonstier

My father lived a full life, and as his daughter, I have many fond memories of him. Most importantly I think that his long life can be attributed to the best description of him as a man, "one who loved and served his fellow man."

He was born on September 24, 1894 to Elizabeth and Thomas Pfisterer of Brodhead, Wisconsin. This twelve pound boy was their eighth child and they named him Thomas, after his father. Tom grew up in this small town and graduated from high school in 1912. He and his brother, Carl, had a burning desire for a college education. They worked at many jobs to pay their tuition, of which the most difficult was raising tobacco. Carl graduated from Beloit College in 1917, while Tom completed two years before enlisting in the army. He trained at Camp Gordon in Atlanta, Georgia. He was then sent overseas with the Field Signal Battalion in France. His battalion saw action in the St. Michiel Drive and at Argonne.

Tragedy struck him when his best friend substituted for him one day when he was ill. His best friend was killed that day. My father's friend had the philosophy that we were all put on this earth to help one another, and that every day we should make an effort toward that end. Tom adopted that as a major part of his lifelong philosophy. Every day he would try to make life count for something and to serve his fellow man.

When he returned from World War I in 1918, he completed his college education, graduated cum laude from Beloit College in 1921. He returned to his hometown to teach math in high school. His strong belief in education and lifelong learning served him and his students well. He and his childhood sweetheart, Dorothy Murphy, were married after his return to Brodhead. They moved to Winslow, Illinois, where he taught and was the school superintendent for eleven years. Two children were born of the marriage, Dr. Tom Pfisterer, currently of Tempe, Arizona and Elsabeth , of Freeport, Illinois.

The Pfisterer family moved to Freeport, Illinois in 1935, where Tom served as the County Superintendent for twenty-four years, before retiring in 1959. He truly loved his teaching and role in education. He was an inspiration to both the students and teachers. He especially looked back with great fondness on the years he spent in Winslow, where everyone knew each other and cared for each other in a small town way.

Tom was also a very community-minded and church (Methodist) oriented person. He was a recipient of the Silver Beaver Award through his involvement with the Boy Scouts of America. He served on the Budget Committee of the Community Chest, while also serving in various capacities for the Salvation Army and the American Legion. Tom reached the level of thirty-second degree Mason, having been an active member of the Masonic Lodge for more than fifty years. His involvement with education did not end with his retirement. My father served for nine years as the President of the Retired Teachers of Stephenson County.

I think the one activity that gave my father the most enjoyment in his later years was visiting the nursing homes, where he was given the nickname, "The Banana Man." One day when he was visiting, a man asked him if he could please bring him a whole banana the next time he came. The man said that all he ever got was little slices of banana in his Jell-O, and before he died, he wanted to eat a whole banana. The idea was born that day to bring bananas to the residents. My father did just that, for ten years, once a week, "The Banana Man" delivered bananas to the nursing home residents.

It was hard to say good-bye to my dad last year, but I like to think he is just as busy in Heaven!

Elsabeth Pfisterer

Enjoy the little things, for one day you may look back and realize that they were big things.

Robert Brault

Remembrance of Grandmother

She was born October 19th, 1905 in her Grandfathers Indiana farmhouse. Grandmother's last conscious moments were in the same farmhouse, where she had raised her four children.

Married right after high school at 17, the first of four children, Russell, was born a year later. It was a struggle to keep the farm going. At least for grandmother, it was. Grandfather was a sociable and intelligent fellow. He enjoyed strolling and fishing and life in general. But not farm work. When the marriage ended, she was left to support her family through the Depression, while trying to keep the farm. Not only was she able to accomplish just that, but she was also determined to see all her children through college. And that is exactly what she did. Russell, though, chose to return from college to run the farm. No handout, no assistance, just sheer will and determination.

She lived for her family. Her life was the family. Grandmother was the embodiment of unconditional love. Though she did not have much, she shared what she had generously with her children and grandchildren alike. Whatever help she could provide, she did.

Whatever little thing you did for her, it was something glorious to grandmother. Whether it was a grandchild moving the cats off the porch, or waiting for her to return home from work and sitting in a mud puddle after tiring from the wait. These were some of the stories long told, of inconsequential things to others, but meaning all the world to her.

If I too am able to seek and glorify the best in others, in the littlest of things, then I will feel that I have learned much, and have returned something of value.

Thank you, grandmother, for your gift of love for all time.

Steve Spyrison

Without heroes we're all plain people and don't know how far we can go.

Bernard Malamud

I Remember Wayne

Mickey Mantle, Al Kaline and Wayne were my heroes when I was growing up. Who was Wayne? He was my idol, my friend, my confidant, and my uncle. Wayne was only six years older than me and was more like a brother, as he and my grandmother lived with us for many years after the death of my grandfather. Wayne would attend the same junior and senior high schools that I would. He was known by the coaches and the teachers and prepared them for me.

Born Delbert Wayne Williams on August 2, 1952, he was always known as Wayne to us. It wasn't unusual for families from West Virginia to name their sons after the father and forever be known by their middle name. I'm well aware of this custom, as I've had the same fate. Wayne's father, Delbert, died when Wayne was only nine. He was the only child of Delbert and Mabel Williams, whose first husband, Jesse, had died a decade earlier from an injury sustained in the mines of West Virginia. Wayne was always considered a part of the Collins' family, despite the difference in the last name. I was probably around eight years old before I realized that I had another grandfather and that Wayne was my mother's step-brother. That was also around the time when Wayne and ma-maw (our name for grandmother) came to live with us.

Wayne and I shared a room. We became soulmates, though not without the territorial brother battles. More often than not, however, we co-conspired to get away with as much as possible. We covered for each other. We competed in sports. He took me to games and events. I can still remember riding the buses to downtown Detroit to see the Tigers play at Michigan and Trumbull. This was also the site of my first professional football game. The Lions and the Cleveland Browns with Jim Brown. The Lions actually won the game! The trip to the Olympia Stadium to see my first hockey game and two of the greatest of all time , Gordie Howe and Bobby Orr, who scored the tying goal with three seconds left in the game. No overtimes in the 1960's. We would go to Cobo Hall to see Dave Bing and the Pistons play my favorite sport, basketball. It didn't matter who was playing. These guys were professional basketball players.

This lead to the endless games of one-on-one in the backyard on the driveway with the nine foot basket. I was always so impressed that Wayne could reach the rim, until I learned that our basket wasn't regulation height. He taught me how to shoot a jump shot, how to dribble with my left hand, and how to angle a bank shot. The ultimate was when Wayne challenged me and my best friend, Carl, to a game of one on two. The loser buys breakfast at the newly opened Morningstar Restaurant. Carl and I practiced for weeks leading up to the game. The game went back and forth. First to ten, had to win by two. Carl and I were up 6-5. Wayne took the lead at 8-7. He got the rebound and could have gone up by two. He missed the bank shot and I ended up with the rebound, passed to Carl behind the check line, and back to me for a lay-up. Tied score! I couldn't believe it when the score was 9-9. Then we went ahead, 10-9. Wayne took his shot from the top of the key. The one he never missed! Clank, off the front of the rim. We had a chance to win! Carl passed to me, back to Carl and then to me at the side, just inbounds along the fence. Wayne ran at me, but I let the shot go just before he got there. Off the backboard, nothing but net. Just like Wayne had taught me! He smiled and playfully ran at both of us. That was probably the best breakfast I ever had and the only time Wayne ever lost to me or the two of us. I still wonder if it was because of motivation for food or Wayne's purposeful "missed" shot? Some day I may find out.

Wayne's high school sports' days were numbered by a "blown-out" knee during his senior year. The knee had to be surgically reconstructed. This was in 1968, during the height of the Vietnam War. Two years later he would fail his physical after being drafted, his mother and his family wept for this unexpected blessing. I can still see Wayne standing proudly along the sidelines on Senior Night with his jersey on, hopping up and down between the yard markers with his crutches in tow. He graduated from Lincoln High School in Warren, Michigan in the spring of 1969. That summer would be the last full summer he would live with us. We drove him to Marquette in the Upper Peninsula of Michigan in August. He was one of the first children to attend college, Northern Michigan University.

He made it through slightly more than one semester. His oldest brother died following an accident in November. Wayne, Bub (another nicknamed uncle), Roy, and I drove back to Michigan through Ohio on our way home from the funeral in West Virginia. We talked about school, about our dreams, and about the family we belonged to. I learned that there was music beyond the Top 40, that it was okay to laugh even after a funeral, that life goes on, and that I was "one of the gang." We even took the daring chance of driving through downtown Columbus,

Ohio with Michigan license plates, as the Wolverines were beating Ohio State in Ann Arbor! Little was I to know, that I was to live through seven more deaths within this family, all but one before their fiftieth birthday.

The next several years are somewhat vague in my memories of Wayne. He lived with us off and on between roommates, various jobs, and attempts at returning to school. Two incidents that I vividly remember were having him come to our celebration party after our freshman football team went undefeated (I had been the starting quarterback) and actually besting him in a basement brawl when I was upset about him drinking too much.

Wayne eventually went to live with his mother, my grandmother, who decided to move back to the family land in Clear Creek, West Virginia. During the summer of 1975, the last break before I would graduate from high school, I stayed with another uncle in Beckley, West Virginia. I had the opportunity to see Wayne throughout that summer. We would walk the backwoods, just like when we were kids. At least he didn't shoot me with the B.B. gun this time. We would spend hours talking out on the front porch, looking into the stars and the mountains. He expressed his regrets for not having completed his higher education and being "stuck" in a job he didn't fully enjoy. He had started smoking, which frustrated him, and he had put on more weight than he cared to admit. He was still the person I looked up to and was the first person I called to go to the Jethro Tull concert at the Charleston Civic Center. When I first found out about album oriented rock music, Wayne had introduced me to their music. I've managed to go to six more of their concerts since. I headed back to Michigan about a week later for the start of my senior year.

We went to West Virginia for Christmas in 1975. It was one of the best ever. I brought my guitar and we sat around the pot belly stove in my great- grandmother's old country home, which still had a well and outhouse, and sang Christmas carols. I can't recall a time before or since that my family sang anything together. We may not have been harmonious, but we were joyful. My cousins' band was playing at a night club that New Year's Eve and the men went to hear them play.

A night out with the guys was a very rare occurrence. Wayne and I even got our first stage experience singing along with the band. Personally , I think they turned off our mikes, but who cared at that point. We were part of a rock and roll band. That is one Christmas holiday I will always remember.

Wayne surprised us all when he drove up to Michigan with a friend the following April. He had just come for a visit. It was just a couple of days. I was busy preparing for graduation. I had a speech to get ready for the big day; one of the honors of being class president. There was much going on and I didn't skip school the morning Wayne asked me to go out to breakfast with him. There would be time for dinner or breakfast later. There's always more time, isn't there? Wayne left that day. He left a note that said he had to get back to work. I didn't get a chance to say good-bye.

My mother and I were out for groceries on the Saturday morning of May 1st. We had taken the car they had bought for me for graduating with honors and receiving a National Merit Scholarship. I couldn't believe that my tuition would be covered throughout all my undergraduate studies. I planned on going to medical school someday. My dad met us at the door with the news. Wayne had been in a serious accident that morning. He had fallen asleep coming home from work. Less than two miles from his home, he went off the side of the road and was thrown through the windshield. His head hit a large rock and he was in a coma. Wayne was transported by ambulance to Charleston Memorial Hospital when there was nothing more they could do in Beckley.

My mother and I left within the hour for Charleston. My dad and sisters would follow the next day. I thought, "That can't be Wayne all hooked up to those tubes with his face swollen." Wayne always seemed indestructible. He came through everything. My mom was distraught. It was as if one of her own children was laying there. We kept a bedside vigil for the rest of the week. Finally, everyone except mom went home. Although the school had been sympathetic and I had enough credits to graduate, I had classes to complete, prom was coming up and I had graduation to attend. People have been known to be in comas for months or years.

My mother took my grandmother to her house during the afternoon of May 10th. It was the first time they had left the hospital. My uncle, Roy, went to the cafeteria for dinner. Left alone at last, Wayne's heart beat its final beat. He had left this world at the age of 23. We would never have the chance to go down to the corner store for a Pepsi, barbeque Fritos and a Suzy-Q, then watch our beloved Red Wings on t.v. again. My soul mate, my confidant, my hero, my uncle was gone and I hadn't had the chance to say good-bye.

I went on to graduate from high school that June and eventually went into medicine. My love of sports lead me into the field of podiatry. I ran track in college and thought of the lessons that Wayne had taught me when he first realized that I had a natural ability to run. I think about him now as I near by fortieth birthday. I wonder what it would have been like had I still been able to confide in him. I still do things in my life with the thought of making him proud of me. I wish my wife and daughters could have met Uncle Wayne. He did teach me that life goes on and you can learn to laugh again, even after a loved one has died. Each day I look toward heaven and thank him for the lessons, thank him for the memories he provided me during his short stay on earth, thank him for being my uncle, and ask that he save a place for me on the basketball court. I'm sure he has a game or two left in him. He may even "let" me win another game.

Roland Tolliver

2

Childhood Memories

We find delight in the beauty and happiness of children that makes the heart too big for the body.

Emerson

To have courage for whatever comes in life-everything lies in that.

St. Teresa of Avila

The Piano Recital

Every spring, Mary Louise Greene hosted a piano recital, featuring all of her students, from kindergarten through twelfth grade. On a Sunday afternoon, mothers, fathers, grandparents, aunts and uncles filled the Durand United Methodist Church, sitting through thirty songs with titles like *Pink Pagoda* or *The Syncopated Clock*, and several works by Bach or Beethoven. Every student memorized his or her solo. Every student wanted to please Mrs. Greene, a wonderfully cheerful and supportive teacher, who treated us all like grandchildren.

My brother, Chris, and I, now in eighth and sixth grades respectively, had worked our way through several years of our own *Crazy Caterpillar*-type songs. This year, he would play Scott Joplin's *The Entertainer*, and I would play Edward Grieg's *Wachterlied*. For the first time, we'd both be performing "real music."

Also for the first time, I was taking my piano solo to the Illinois High School Solo and Ensemble Contest. I would also take a flute solo and a flute duet to the contest, which was scheduled one week prior to Mrs. Greene's piano recital. The solo and ensemble contest was causing more than a little friction in my home. Even as a sixth-grader, I had a need to be perfect. My solos and duet couldn't be just okay; every note of every phrase had to be just so. I knew that if I didn't get first-place ratings for the solos and duet, I would not be able to face my friends and family. During the weeks leading up to the day of the contest, my stress spread to the rest of my family.

The piano solo had to be completely memorized. As Mrs. Greene suggested, I learned four or five starting spots in the song, so if I lost my place, I'd be able to jump ahead to some logical point. Whenever I played from memory, I'd see the pages of sheet music in my mind, and know what page and line I was playing at any given time. It was important to concentrate on the music at every second of the performance.

Luckily, all went well at the solo and ensemble contest. I received first-place medals for all three events, and was able to hold my head up in sixth-grade band. I relaxed.

The day of Mrs. Greene's piano recital came a week later. I didn't worry too much, because I had played my piece pretty well the previous Saturday. Mom, Dad, Aunt Jennifer, Uncle John, and two cousins sat in the pews of the church. Every pew was full of relatives and friends of all of the piano students. Chris sat next to me in the pews at the front, which were turned to the audience so parents could see their children all dressed up in their Sunday best.

One by one, Mrs. Greene presented the students. Each student would introduce his or her solo, then play the piece. The students had rehearsed their introductions, as well as the little bow made after solos, during their lessons at Mrs. Greene's farm during the weeks before the recital.

When Mrs. Greene introduced me, she added, "We're so proud of Becky, because she received a perfect score on this solo at the Illinois High School Solo and Ensemble Contest last week." What an introduction to live up to! Everyone knew I'd played perfectly a week earlier — what if I didn't play perfectly now? What if I made a mistake?!

I introduced my solo (making sure to say "v" instead of "w" in Edward Grieg and *Wachterlied*) and sat at the piano. Concentration was the key to remembering what note came next. As Mrs. Greene had instructed, I collected my thoughts for a moment before beginning. My fingers had a mind of their own, and I flew through the first section. I started enjoying myself. It was fun to play in front of people! Then my mind started wandering, and I abruptly stopped playing. I hadn't followed the music on the page in my mind, and I couldn't remember what came next. So I took a deep breath , and began playing at one of the points in the song that was memorized especially for this purpose. Unfortunately I selected a spot that was earlier in the song. When I came to the trouble spot for the second time, I was still unable to remember what came next. I sat there for a moment then looked up at Mrs. Greene. She walked to the piano and put her arms around my shoulders. She kindly directed me back to the student section.

I sat and listened to the other children play their solos. Everyone made it through their pieces, with not more than a few minor problems. Chris wowed the audience with *The Entertainer*. I tried not to cry, but it was very hard. Luckily, somebody passed me a tissue. I wasn't perfect! I had failed — in front of my family and about 200 other people! At eleven years old, I was a failure.

Everyone else was done playing. Mrs. Greene looked at me with a question in her eyes, and I nodded my head. I walked over to the piano and sat down. I still wasn't sure what I had done wrong the first time, but I was ready to try again. I started playing. As I drew closer to the trouble spot, I became more and more nervous. Once again, I drew a blank when I came to that measure. This time, instead of stopping, I just played through it. I fudged a few measures until I got back on steady footing. Although it was far from perfect, I made it through the song. Everyone applauded and Mrs. Greene thanked everyone for coming.

When Chris and I met up with our family after the recital, I could tell that Mom had been crying. That wasn't surprising, because Mom cried at the drop of a hat. But, when I noticed that Aunt Jennifer had been crying too, I was puzzled. Mom hugged me and said, "Oh, Becky. We're so proud of you! I would never have been able to get up there and try again!" When I asked why they had cried, Aunt Jennifer told me, "I think every woman in the church cried. We all felt so bad for you, and then we were so proud of you for playing a second time." Other women, some whom I didn't even know, also hugged me and told me they were proud of me.

I don't know if it's the bravest thing I ever did, but sitting down at the piano for the second time certainly taught me a lot about myself. I had to admit that I couldn't always be perfect, and that it's okay just to do your best. I learned that a failure could be turned into a success, especially in the eyes of my family.

In spite of these valuable lessons, I hope I never again make a church full of women cry.

Becky Connors

On Second Thought, I'll have the Meatloaf

Once, a very long time ago, I got stuck in a hen house. I was staying at my grandfather's farm for a couple of weeks in the summer and I was a very curious four-year-old. Just the week before I had wandered off with the sheep and scared everyone half to death until I wandered back with them. And now I was fascinated by the chickens—so much so that one day I followed them right into their living quarters.

I'm not sure how I got through the tiny door they used, but I somehow managed to pop across and now there I was inside the hot, smelly hen house. As my eyes got used to the dim light, I saw that I was surrounded by chickens—and not just regular chickens but giants, ten feet high who stalked around with their golden eyes flashing angrily while they clucked chicken threats at me.

Terrified, I tried to get back out through that same little door but I must have swollen up because I couldn't do it, no matter how hard I tried. I pushed at the big door—no good — it was fastened on the outside. There was only one thing to do so I started screaming at noon-whistle volume. After several moments, the latch rattled and there was my Grandpa Jack standing in the light of the doorway. I sobbed against his comforting stomach. He lifted me up and talked away my tears as only he could do — he was that kind of a grandfather.

Eventually, I calmed down but you can bet I never tried that little door again — in fact for the rest of the vacation I gave the whole hen yard a wide berth. To this day, I'm not really that crazy about chicken.

Rick Mosher

Childhood is the kingdom where nobody dies.

Edna St. Vincent Millay

Empty Tracks

When Alane, Andra, and Ashly's Grandpa Lane died, the family traveled from Illinois back to Mediapolis, Iowa. As the family crossed the railroad tracks a mile out of town, their mother reminded them that Grandpa wouldn't be there in his chair like he had always been. She told them that he had gone to Heaven to be with God. She asked them to try and remember not to ask Grandma where he was, because that might upset her and make her feel bad.

Ashly, the three year old, reminded the family about this during every trip back to Iowa for the next year. Whenever we crossed the railroad tracks, he would remind everyone that Grandpa's chair would still be there, but it would be *empty*. He then reminded us not to ask Grandma where Grandpa was, "cause we don't want Grandma to feel bad!"

Our childhoods are shaped by our memories of those living and deceased. Our courtesies are learned from those we love. May we never stop learning and may we never stop teaching our children about those we love.

Leola Brechtel

Laura's Mother

"How many would you like?" Mother would ask this as she deftly poured her own pancake batter into the cast iron pan—pancakes that were thin, golden brown and big. As a child, three or four pancakes were not enough when filled and rolled with the thick, sweetened whipped cream that was delivered to our house–country fresh–the real thing.

Mother was an excellent cook so nothing went to waste–especially because we lived through the hard times of the Depression.

Our house was always filled with people–friends, family, and relatives. There was always room at the table for anyone to join us in our meals and love, compassion and generosity to anyone who needed it.

In her last years, mother was bedridden because of a terminal illness. Still the house was always filled with people who were concerned about mother. She could no longer cook to prepare her delicious food, so we knew that was not the only reason the house was always filled. It was because mother was such a loving, caring person.

I'm now approaching the age mother was when she became ill. Our seven children are grown and have made their own lives. They have given us eight lovely grandchildren. Our home is a gathering place for them and they all keep in touch. I'd like to think that some of mother's qualities have passed onto me to carry out her traditions.

Thank you, Mother. I love you.

Laura Carlson (copyright)

We Need One Another

This is a true story of me at thirteen years of age and in the seventh grade of our public school in Indiana. It was a civics class and also physiology in which we were discussing that food, clothing and shelter were necessities for human life.

All at once I raised my hand. When the teacher called upon me I answered, "we also have to have one another." Oh, you should have heard the laughing—especially the boys of my age of thirteen and fourteen years. I was so embarrassed and wished I hadn't said it.

However, "We have to have one another" is so true in our lives. Since I grew to maturity, entered the field of teaching for thirty-nine years, married a wonderful man in Freeport, and am now in my eighty-seventh year of age, I know how much we need each other.

Charlotte Zartman

Grandfathers:
In Honor of Dave

Grandfathers are very special people
and they are really very neat.

They take you to ballgames, golf and fishing
and give you candy even when Mom says no sweets.

Grandfathers are there to lend you money
and then softens up grandma by saying ah, Honey...

They have a way of brightening up your darkest day
by just saying that's really okay.

Even when your hot dog falls out of the bun
He can still say with a smile your my favorite grandson.

He'll take you out fishing next to a nice little brook
and ends up half of the day baiting the end of your hook.

Grandfathers always have a listening ear
and help you calm your greatest fear.

They're there to cheer you and make you feel glad
and usually don't shout even when you're sometimes bad.

One of the greatest gifts sent from above
is to have a child know their grandfather's love.

Whether your grandfather be short or tall
I hope you think your grandfather is the best of all!

Vicky Busker

Ellen

Another Sunday afternoon at Ellen's as I sit on the oriental carpeting and look up to her in her rocking chair. She is propped up with pillows and wearing her usual wool skirt; I scratch my leg...As we begin to talk, my Nana and Ellen and I, I notice that Ellen is bit withdrawn. There are no stories of the Rockefellers or New England today. My conversation with Nana half-heartedly continues as I watch the old woman. Her forehead wrinkles, her eyes retreat, and the flush to her face grows brighter. Suddenly the phone rings and everyone is startled for a moment. We let it ring for a long while before Nana answers and hands it to Ellen. There is much fidgeting while Ellen struggles to remove her hearing aid and finally speaks. She talks slowly for some time in her comforting, old knowledgeable voice and then rests the receiver back upon its cradle. She purses her lips, sighs, and attempts to insert the hearing aid. Finally, she motions to her "sitter" and her hearing aid is ground back into her ear. Nana and I babble on and then we stand to leave. The walker is again placed in front of her and she is snapped back to reality long enough to say goodbye, hold out her hand, and let me kiss her cheek. I leave her feeling warm, knowing that she is forever sitting in her chair, contemplating...Ellen is supreme.

Karyla K. Trester (Copyright)

Fay Cole

Fay Cole: tiny and unpretentious as her name; quick and restless as a wren. Her frown was not of disapproval, but of eager concentration; her laugh was not so much a voiced sound, as a twinkle of mutual pleasure. Miss Cole was my fourth grade teacher.

Year nine, grade four is said to be developmentally exciting for every child. Miss Cole made it magic. We wrote "personal essays," not just "about something," and I fell in love with the semicolon. She pulled books out of her cabinet. Easy books like *Poppy Seed Cakes*, we read; strange and lovely ones like *Shen of the Sea*, she read aloud.

And we sang—how we sang that year. With our green music books tucked under our arms we marched up to the third floor auditorium to the piano, and roared out "If ever you should go by chance to jungles in the East... Vittoria, Vittoria, Swedley wee...!" and a bird sound song, "Whip-por-will, Chicka-dee-ee-ee, Bob-bob Whi-ite..." Best of all, she taught us part singing; I first heard the thirds and sixths that have made being an alto such a lifelong joy.

Each child had big roles and small roles. If you lead one event, you might be on the cleanup for the next. We did our own elaborate production of "Hansel and Gretel," and though I longed with all my heart to be Gretel, curly blonde Gloria Ann got that part. Miss Cole convinced me that my leading the dance of the eight gingerbread boys was important to the whole class; I believed her. Later she told me I "stole the show;" I believed that, too.

Sometimes, at the end of "such a good day," Miss Cole went to the glass-fronted cabinet (with pretty wallpaper behind the glass, to keep its secrets) and brought forth some plain Hershey bars. On a little piece of paper on each desk, she carefully placed one little square of chocolate. We waited until all were served, then, those last few minutes of that good day, each licked slowly, meltingly, lovingly, we tasted Miss Cole's magical understanding.

Barbara S. Moody

There are no elements so diverse that they cannot be joined in the heart of a man or woman.

Jean Giraudoux

Father Kalvelage

In this, the autumn of my life, events which had an impact on my upbringing are good to remember.

As a child I lived on Broadway, between Oak and Walnut, a large block. About the age of 5, I was allowed to push my doll buggy around that block. (Things were much simpler, as well as safer, then.)

Each morning as I took my doll (with "real " hair) in my brown wicker doll buggy, down Broadway, over Walnut to Pleasant, Father Kalvelage (later the Right Reverend Monseigneur) was walking behind St. Joseph's Church while reading his prayer book. Seeing me across the street, he would hesitate a moment and ask how my baby was.

When I would get home, I would tell my mom the nice man in the long black coat asked about my doll baby.

Each time my mother would patiently explain to me that he was the pastor of that large Catholic church.

At first this was a puzzlement to me, for you see I went to the Presbyterian Sunday School, and the pastor there wore a business suit just like my dad.

This is how I learned at a very early age that people might dress differently, but that we're all pretty much the same underneath.

Henrietta Wurtzel

On Thanksgiving Day

I'm thankful for the distant hum
Of trucks and motor cars,
For honking geese, for blizzard winds
For twinkling of the stars.

I'm thankful for the voice of rain
Upon the thirsty earth.
Such blessings, although common-place
Are blessings of great worth.

They bring a joy and inner peace
That linger in my soul.
To God I offer thanks EACH day
For these have made me whole.

Vera Emmert Johansen

Unto the pure all things are pure.

Titus 1:15

Show and Tell

When Barb and Larry Fiene's daughter, Teresa, was in kindergarten her grandfather passed away. She was absent from school for several days. The day she returned was "Show and Tell." She was called up to present her "show and tell" to the class. With her little lisp, she explained to all of us about how her grandpa died.

"He went up to live in Heaven. They put him in a very special box, like a big basket. There was a special soft pillow for his head. It was so-o-o beautiful. He had his hands folded like this." She demonstrated with her tiny hands in front of the class, then continued.

"He just looked so peaceful. He looked like he was sleeping!"

She then told her classmates, who were spellbound, "The flowers were all pretty and there were so many. It looked just like a BIG garden!"

The class applauded as she sat down. Most of the students had not yet experienced the death of a loved one. Teresa had put into plain language what she had seen and felt at her grandfather's funeral.

When you look through the eyes of a child and listen to their words, you experience their feelings and simple faith. Sometimes we need to follow the example of a child's "Show and Tell," to know God's wisdom and beauty

Barbara Fiene

Mother's Smile

Mother, I saw your smile today,
Your reflection in me as I went on my way,
The mirror caught that sparkle and gleam,
It lasted a moment, so it would seem.

I miss your hand to dry away tears,
Words of encouragement to erase all my fears,
The look of worry when things go amiss,
The love and concern that come with a kiss.

But, now I'll be happy, perhaps sing a song,
God sent a message to carry along.
My mirrored-image paused to pray,
For Mother, I saw your smile today.

Joan H. Kruse (copyright)

Children are the true connoisseurs. What's precious to them has no price-only value.

Bel Kaufman

A Child's Love
is Parents'
Best Christmas Gift

With Christmastime upon us, I find myself faced with the annual dilemma as to what to give the two most influential people in my life – my parents. Just what on God's green Earth is appropriate for the people who have given me the ultimate in gifts, I don't know.

Ever since the late, but revered Dr. John Linden delivered me into this world at then St. Francis Hospital, my folks have more than held up their end of the bargain. My only wish is that it wouldn't have taken me so many years to become appreciative for the job they continue doing to this day.

Although my name and words appear in the newspaper on a semi-regular basis, my father is much better known throughout the area than I could hope to be. His notoriety as a high school sports official has been earned by decades of dedication, the number of people with whom he has shared a court or field of play would be incalculable. I cannot think of one area school where he has not worked many a contest.

If you think it is difficult to watch a family member compete in a sporting event, you ought to try and watch them umpire or referee. No one in attendance seems to like them. Nowadays, poor losers can even use videotape with pinpoint angles and slow motion replays to prove your loved one guilty of making a mistake. Sportscasters concerned more with hype than ethics spread the news with zest.

While some of my father's experience may be painful, perhaps humiliating, it has not come without rewards. It has taught me all about making judgment calls, then living with the decision. It has shown me that absolute fairness, though usually unobtainable, is an ideal worth striving for. Like perfection, absolute fairness in human endeavors doesn't occur often, if ever. This does not mean we should stop trying. Our efforts will surely be taken into consideration by the Final Judge.

My mother could be described very well using just one word. Devotion. I have yet to meet anyone with more to offer than Mom. Five siblings and I pulled her in every direction, figuratively and literally. I can recall one year that due to the family's geographical location she had elementary school Christmas programs to attend in three different towns, Baileyville, German Valley and Forreston. Keeping up with the interest and needs of six ceaselessly growing and experimenting kids is not an easy job. Anyone who thinks it is has not been there.

Now that her children have all reached adulthood doesn't necessarily mean a reduction in responsibility, just different ways of applying it. I don't believe a mother's basic fears and desires can be alleviated simply by the passing of time.

By example Mom taught me to think for myself. I will never forget a Chicago Cubs game in August, 1984. It was a critical doubleheader against the hated New York Mets. During the second game a benchclearing brawl erupted sending the 40,000 Wrigley Field faithful into a frenzy. While everyone else in the ballpark stood and chanted in unison, Mom sat quietly in her terrace reserved seat reading a book she had brought from home. When I questioned her on her lack of emotion she told me nothing happening on the field that day would affect her future. While peer pressure might be real, Mother proved to me you don't have to succumb to it. Had I taken this lesson more seriously earlier in life I could have saved myself much embarrassment.

As a teen-ager in the wide open 1970's the only thing that concerned me was immediate gratification. For a long time my horizons remained dangerously narrow, through the shameful and the tragic my parents continued to offer me all the love and nurturing at their disposal. Shortly before my 30th birthday their patient perseverance paid off. Unfortunately the past cannot be replaced regardless of remorse.

Whatever I decide to wrap up and place under the Christmas tree, it won't be able to compare in value with what my parents have given me. I just hope I find something that they can enjoy throughout the coming year. Heaven knows I've already given them enough to endure.

John S. Cook

3

Joys of Parenting

Continue to look at your children as valuable treasures. Honor them and yourself.

Bernie Siegel

Somehow we learn who we really are and then live with that decision.

Eleanor Roosevelt

Such a Tiny Person; Such a Big Decision

Babies are such tiny things, as older, bigger people are prone to note. "Oooooh, what itty-bitty hands," they gush. "Oh, my. Look at those little feet. I love that little nose."

But somehow, the seven- or eight-pound bundle of miniature features looms incredibly large - resulting in a total eclipse of the parents, despite their superior motor development. People who used to start conversations with "How are you?" have traded the phrase for "How's the baby?" But do we as parents then feel shunned, rejected, resentful, passed over? Of course not - because our lives, too, have become completely absorbed by this diaper-clad, roly-poly being and our only regret is that the questioner does not have 30 to 40 minutes longer to listen to us speak ad nauseam about our child's latest accomplishment, which in the early weeks usually involves poop.

I have been one such parent for about 3 months now and I have yet to tire of answering the question as I will now demonstrate: The baby is fine, beautiful and delightful.

Jane Elizabeth, who was born at a scant 2 pounds 10 ounces in April, is thriving and growing, and on Wednesday tipped the scales at a whopping 8 pounds 13 ounces. She's still small enough at 3 months to cause people who know nothing about her premature birth to look at me askance as if wondering (but afraid to ask), "Do you feed her?" but boy, do I feed her. She eats vigorously and often, which has helped her grow from a frighteningly small preemie tucked protectively in an Isolette to a healthy, chubby person with the whole baby act down pat. She does poop, but I won't go into that. She clings charmingly to fingers and reaches for toys. Her cheeks are chubby; her elbows are dimpled. She can almost hold her head up. She smiles, she coos and she stares with fascinated wonder at the faces of the big people who hang over her, burbling baby talk.

She knows just when to smile, to make the little surprised face with the big eyes and the pursed lips, just when to wave those little hands at admiring fans. My husband calls it "turning on the cute motor." If she plays to her audience this well now, what are we in for when she's 14?

You know, in the months before a person adds parenthood to their life resume, everyone (and I mean everyone) who has gone before into this great adventure will say, "Your life will never be the same." I believed that, I really did, but I think the reality is that there is no way for any person to understand the depth and breadth of that truth until that small cry breaks the silence of the house at 4 a.m. I have never felt a stronger compulsion to do anything than to comfort Jane. I have never felt so happy as when I kiss that tiny, fuzzy head. I have never felt more alive as when she is spread-eagled across my chest.

I have for many years asserted to people that I would be, must necessarily be, a working mother. I don't have the temperament to stay at home with a child, I proclaimed. I need the stimulation of the work-a-day world, I insisted. I'd be a better part-time mother than a full-time mother, I explained airily.

Hey, I've been wrong before.

Since the time Jane was born on April 20 and even more since she came home on June 10, she has worked on me in mysterious ways. About three weeks before the end of my maternity leave, I realized I did not want to go back to work. I did not want Jane to spend her days in day care. I wanted her to spend her days with me.

"Too bad," was my first reaction to myself. "You have to work, Jane needs her mother, but she also needs a roof over her head, some clothes and a meal here and there."

But the wheels kept turning, greased by advice and support from people who know about things like working from home as a freelance writer. The wheels turned so far, they turned me around. Last week I told my friends at the Journal-Standard that I would not remain with them as a full-time member of the news gathering team. They have been gracious enough to allow me to keep the connection through this weekly column and through other occasional assignments.

It took some thought. There's a lot I'll miss by staying at home. I loved my job and the people I came to know because of it. The security of a regular paycheck is nice. But there are more important things I'd miss in Jane's life by staying at work. Being a writer gives me a choice many people wouldn't have. It's a precious gift and when one is given a gift, is it not most gracious to accept?

So for the first time, I'm writing a column not in the office, but at home. My sleeping daughter is a few feet away. I don't think life has ever felt so close to perfect.

Sonja Somerville

Calves in the Kitchen & Pigs on the Stove

It was nine A.M., and already it had been a long day. My day had started at 5 A.M. when I leaped out of bed to the shout of, "Honey, that heifer's calving early. I need your help!" As I tried to focus my eyes, I automatically pulled on my long johns, sweatshirt, two pairs of socks, coveralls, boots, hat, scarf, and mittens, and waddled out the door.

Of course, it was sleeting. Of course, the heifer had chosen to calve in the corner farthest from the barn. Of course, she was lying on a sea of mud and manure, and of course, I fell in it.

The heifer calved with little trouble, but refused to nurse the calf. So it was carried to the house for warmth and a bottle. I layed the calf on an old braided rug by the old stove, rubbed it dry, and gave it a bottle of milk.

I had just peeled off my wet and slimy coveralls, two pairs of socks, hat, mittens, scarf, and long johns, gotten into a warm, dry, quilted robe, and sat down with a hot cup of coffee, when a familiar voice hollered, "Honey, the sows are starting to farrow!" Off went the warm quilted robe, back into the pot went the hot coffee, and back on went the wet and slimy work clothes.

The sows gave birth to little pigs in rapid succession, but one had fourteen piglets and only twelve dinner plates. These extra piglets were mine to raise by bottle. So into the house for extra care came two runt pigs. Since the calf had an honoured place by the stove, the piglets were wrapped in an old flannel baby blanket and placed in a box on the warmed oven.

Off again came the wet, slimy frozen overalls, hat, scarf, mittens, two pairs of socks, and long johns. On went the warm quilted robe, and once again I sank into a chair with a hot cup of coffee, hoping to be able to finish it this time.

I looked around my cozy farm kitchen. The calf was struggling to stand, the piglets wiggled in their blanket making soft noises of happiness, and my children upstairs fought as they started their morning rituals. I sat there tired, but content to have this peaceful moment to myself. Others, I thought, may have fancy cars, furs, and jewels, but I have calves in my kitchen and pigs on my stove.

Dianne Walters-Butler (copyright)

The love we give away is the only love we keep.

Elbert Hubbard

Savannah Smiles

My daughter, Sharla, and granddaughter, Savannah, were shopping one evening in a local grocery store, which had small carts for the children. Savannah decided that she wanted to "shop too."

Sharla was moving right along. Savannah, having had a rough day at the babysitter's, was continually moving in front of her mother and stopping in her path. Sharla let this pass several times before her patience started to wear thin.

"Savannah, you have to keep going."

Savannah didn't respond and several more times she stopped in front of her mother.

"Savannah, you have to keep going."

Exasperated by her mother's repeated admonishments, Savannah turned to her mother and said, "But Mom, I can't keep going and going like the pink bunny keeps going and going, you know!"

Mom stopped in her tracks. After she had stopped laughing, she realized that their time together was indeed precious. Mom slowed down so that Savannah could keep up and they continued their shopping together, side by side.

Some days we just have to slow down and appreciate the gift that our children truly are. Our love is the only thing that should keep "going and going."

Betty Hepler

God could not be everywhere so He made mothers.

Arab Proverb

A MOTHER'S SNEAKY INFLUENCE

All mothers influence their children's lives in various ways. Mine gave me freckles and dimples through her genes. Her attitudes, beliefs, examples, and physical care all molded and shaped me into what I was to become as an adult. It was one specific and sneaky decision she made on my behalf that radically shaped my entire life.

During the years from 1935 through 1947 while I attended school in Decatur, Illinois, I always knew that education beyond high school was expected. I was not however, in any hurry to decide what it would be and had nothing particular in mind.

When high school graduation was looming it became urgent to decide what to do and where to do it. Brochures from various colleges began arriving and among them were several from schools of nursing in central Illinois. My decision to apply to Julia F. Barnham School of Nursing in Champaign, Illinois, was based upon several factors. I liked the science courses in high school, the tuition was within an affordable range, I wanted to go away from Decatur (but not too far) and I was dating a Decatur boy, who was attending the U of I in Champaign.

I was accepted into the program and progressed to the first mile marker, "Capping." After six months in school, student nurses receive their cap, which is an earned rite of passage that establishes your desire to continue and the school's acceptance of your abilities.

Shortly after "Capping," my mother confessed she had sent for the brochures from nursing schools. She had always thought I would be a good nurse, but was hesitant to suggest it directly to me, knowing that the rebellious teenager would probably reject the idea.

Between 1947 and 1950 I completed nursing school, met and married my husband, and moved to Freeport, Illinois. I worked in the nursing profession either full or part-time from 1950 until retirement in 1991.

It is hard to imagine what my life would have been if my mother hadn't influenced me in the way she did.

I've never been sorry for her sneakiness.

The following is the family prayer my mother, Edna E. Moody, wrote in June of 1947 as I graduated from high school and my sister graduated from college.

Our Heavenly Father we thank Thee for this period in our home life, for this time of rejoicing, for thought, for future plans. We thank Thee that Thou hast helped us through the years leading to these two events.

Forgive us, we pray, if we have at times neglected to seek Thy guidance and perhaps have made mistakes. We thank Thee for seeing us through hard places. We thank Thee for our daughters whom we love, for their persistence, pluck and achievement in the face of difficulties. We thank Thee for their lovely graduation days, for the love, good wishes and gifts of relatives and friends.

As we thank Thee we also ask Thy further help and guidance in decisions and plans for the future.

May this Commencement of a new period in our girls' lives be as satisfactory as their present completions. May their foundations of home, school and church life be strong enough to help them in everything they may do. Help them to remember that education leads to a fuller life and that service to others and to Thee constitutes the highest type of living.

May we, as parents, give advice when it is needed; silence when that is best, but may we always love and cherish our girls.

Again, our Lord, we thank Thee for these two happy graduation days and we commit our girls and their futures into Thy hands.

AMEN

Carolyn Moody LeBaron

In the sheltered simplicity of the first few days after a baby is born, one sees again the magical closed circle, the miraculousness of two people existing only for each other.

Anne Morrow Lindbergh

The Comforts of Home

Candlelight and soft music greeted Teresa Maria Tolliver, the first baby born in Stephenson County in 1997. The 8- pound, 10-ounce baby girl was born in her parents' bedroom slightly before 6 a.m. Wednesday, New Year's Day.

Teresa's parents, Roland, a podiatrist, and Irena Tolliver, prefer having all of the comforts of home at their fingertips when it's time to add a child to their growing family. Three of their four daughters have now been born at home.

Mrs. Tolliver said being at home in familiar surroundings and seeing a lot of friendly faces is far less stressful than having to be shuttled to, from, and around a hospital.

"It was almost like being romanced by my husband," Mrs. Tolliver said. "except that I had to do the hard work."

The comforts of home provide a more intimate setting than the one she experienced in a hospital, where her oldest child, Mary, was born. Intravenous fluids were provided, she was transferred from room to room on a gurney, and the delivery schedule was controlled by doctors and nurses, rather than by nature, she recalled. She and her husband decided after the first experience that home birth would be a better alternative for them. Home delivery, they felt, was more than a medical phenomenon.

"Giving birth is much more than a physical experience," Mrs. Tolliver said while Teresa was napping, cradled in her mother's arms. "It's an emotional, spiritual experience. Birth is a part of the circle of life. Sometimes that experience cannot be shared in some environments. At home we can do everything together; nobody has to be separated."

Two midwives provided much of the prenatal care for Irena. They served as the primary care-givers after the delivery for mother and daughter. The three older sisters, Mary, 9, Veronica, 7, and Claire, 3, were able to be in mom and dad's bedroom as their sister came into the world. A local physician served as back up to the midwives and would have been available had complications arisen during labor or delivery

The couple was well prepared for home delivery. They had met with doctors who specialize in homebirths, read multiple books on the subject, and took two extensive courses to prepare for pregnancy, labor and delivery. The Tollivers continued to read the latest material on home birthing and worked very closely with their midwives.

"It is an advantage having a midwife, who is a mother herself. She understands labor and instinctively knows when and how to comfort me," Mrs. Tolliver said. It has only been within this century that hospitals have become the primary destination of mothers-to-be. Women managed to give birth without the aid of hospitals for thousands of years, and most still can.

"Most people do feel more secure in a hospital, just in case something goes wrong, and people have become accustomed to it," Dr. Tolliver said. "It would be nice if midwives were better incorporated in the medical community." He cautioned there are times when a hospital environment is the best for the health of all concerned.

Many medical insurance companies are now paying for the costs associated with midwives. The growing interest in having a baby at home prompted many hospitals to make their delivery rooms look and feel more like home, but there is no substitute. "You can't get much more like home, than home,"related Tolliver.

Parents or parents-to-be must take a proactive approach to having their baby at home, as it takes a lot of hard work to prepare everyone concerned. "It takes more work. You have to take the initiative and accept the risks," Mrs. Tolliver said. "It's right for some people but not for everyone."

When describing her recent twelve hours of labor, Mrs. Tolliver used such words as "quiet" and "easy."The period immediately following labor is important, as well. Moments after Teresa was born, she was placed on her mother's abdomen and began breast feeding within two minutes. Not only did mother and child have time to bond, but Mrs. Tolliver said Teresa and her three sisters were able to meet and share some quiet time with the infant. "I think having the girls there helps with the bonding process. Each time I have a baby at home it's different, because there is one more child with us," she said.

Teresa was examined, weighed and measured and given a clean bill of health. One of the midwives came by for a follow-up visit with mother and child on the next day and will return in a week . Mrs. Tolliver said Teresa has been resting comfortably and quietly in the first day- and-a-half of her life. Mrs. Tolliver pulled up her tiny knitted cap and revealed a thick head of black hair, which Dr. Tolliver looked at wistfully. Mom is doing all right too. "I feel very refreshed," Mrs. Tolliver said.

It didn't seem to matter to the Tollivers that Teresa came into their lives on a particular day at a particular time , what was important was that she had arrived. "What greater gift can you have than a healthy baby," Mrs. Tolliver said as she held Teresa close. What greater gift indeed!

Gregory Douglas

Peanut Butter Hugs

I can't name a date on the calendar when I began to see it happening, but it happened just the same.

I saw it coming one day, when I found myself aching for a hug. Running into my arms, my three year old obliged me with delight. Smelling of peanut butter, she wrapped those soft, chubby little arms around my neck. "I love you, Mommy," she whispered into my ear. My heart jumped. It happened.

I've heard it in the "I hope I gross you out" chuckle of my dirty nine year old as he describes the gruesome details of the cat eating a gopher. And knowing he succeeded made it happen again.

I recognize it in the toothless grin of my seven year old daughter as she presents me with a dandelion as if it were gold. Knowing it is, helps me to remember, again.

I watch it happening on the children's faces as we celebrate them–on their birthdays, that keep coming more quickly, one after another, year after year and in their eyes in those moments when mother and child really connect with a knowing, binding love. It certainly happens then.

It happens when I slip in between the cool sheets after a demanding, yet rewarding, day. As I close my eyes to rest, I know the children are tucked in their cozy beds, loved and safe.

I've felt it happen when he calls and asks. "How's your day going, Hon?" Even more when he adds sincerely, "I miss you." And my parents bring it to my heart again and again with their supporting words of encouragement and their ever abiding faith in me.

I'm reminded of it in the blue–so blue–of the sky, filled with clouds so incredibly beautiful that only heaven could have painted them for me. And it happens again as I delight in learning to make things grow, and I know it's there when I find myself squealing like a child when a lovely new pink rose appears.

I've often clung to it in the struggles that resolve easily and in the struggles that require much more effort, especially in those that demand huge amounts of faith to endure. It's there.

I've been challenged by it in the painful times that eventually changed to better times. The triumphs of daily living, --seeing each grow, learn and love, brings it about.

The knowing–the knowing that life is to be cherished in its tender moments, as well as in its most difficult moments. Each to be smelled, caressed, tasted, listened to and experienced for its preciousness and for the fleeting opportunities it brings. Each moment is as unique as we are. Each brings growth and life.

Especially, the Peanut Butter hugs.

Debra Royle Bassett (copyright)

We need four hugs a day for survival;
We need eight hugs a day for health; and
We need twelve hugs a day for optimal health.

Hugs

It's wondrous what a hug can do.
A hug can cheer you when you're blue.
A hug can say "I love you so."
A hug is "Welcome back again."
And "Great to see you! Where have you been?"
A hug can soothe a small child's pain.
And bring a rainbow after the rain.
The hug, there's just no doubt about it —
We scarcely could survive without it!
A hug delights and warms and charms,
It must be why God gave us arms.
Hugs are great for fathers and mothers,
Sweet for sisters, swell for brothers;
And chances are your favorite aunts
Love them more than potted plants.
Kittens crave them, puppies love them;
Heads of states are not above them;
A hug can break, the language barrier,
And make travel so much merrier.
No need to fret about your store of 'em;
The more you give, the more there's of 'em.
So stretch those arms without delay
And give someone a hug today!

Author Unknown
Submitted by: Sophia Spaid

A HUG FOR ALL REASONS

A GOOD HUG CAN HELP YOU BEAR ANYTHING

The A-Frame Hug   Cheek Hug   Heart-Centered Hug   Back-To-Front Hug

Children are the anchors that hold a mother to life.

Sophocles

One Small Miracle

As the weeks and months progressed during the pregnancy of our second child, I had developed an increasingly uneasy feeling. Having miscarried previously, and when the physician had difficulty in hearing the baby's heartbeat, I grew more concerned. Though all the medical tests seemed to show everything to be normal, they did not allay my feelings.

For the most part I continued to feel well and worked every day. I certainly was more comfortable this time, no sciatic pain, even late in the pregnancy. But I would look at myself in the mirror and wonder about the size of the child I carried. I realized that I did not look very big and kept wondering about how small this child might be.

I continued to take great pleasure from our first son, Benjamin, who was under two, and kept me busy and happy. I marveled at my good fortune in being blessed with a caring, loving husband and having a healthy, wonderful son.

As the due date approached, an amniocentesis was scheduled to check on the status of the baby's lungs. The night before, however, I went into labor. Driving myself to the hospital around midnight to see if I really was starting labor, Steve stayed home to care for Ben. At the hospital the contractions became more intense and I phoned Steve to hurry over as the birth appeared to be fast approaching.

It seemed as though the next series of events was happening to someone else, that I was just the observer. In a matter of a very short time it was clear that something was seriously wrong. I was readied for an emergency C-Section very quickly. As an oxygen mask was being placed on my face, the physicians and nurses were literally running to get me as quickly as possible to the operating room. As I lay on the rapidly moving cart, I remember thinking practically that this could not be happening to me. I have seen this hundreds of times in my work as a recovery room nurse. I have been a part of this from the other side. How could this be happening to me?

I remember very little until much later when awakened from the anesthetic. I vaguely recall looking through the sides of an isolette at my very tiny newborn son before he was transferred to the Rockford Neonatal Intensive Care. I was just relieved that he was alive. Later, a nurse who was a friend and had helped care for me would relate the despair and hopelessness that was present among the staff as Tyler was born. Steve commented on the expression when the physician tried to relay what had happened, that his look bore the weight of responsibility for that which is not always in our control - the responsibility of those choices that are made not from this world.

I would learn later that Tyler's Apgar score, usually 7-10 which relates to the infant's condition at birth, was 0. He was not breathing on his own and had to have a breathing tube inserted and be resuscitated.

Strangely as the days went on, I did not worry about Tyler's outcome. Somehow, I had an instinctive feeling that he would be all right. Though later, Steve, my sister and parents would express that they were concerned minute by minute and had no such intuition as did I. Each day the pediatrician would faithfully call me and give the latest update on Tyler's condition. Tyler continued to hold his own and show steady improvement, though his weight had dropped to under 3 pounds for days.

Steve would comment on his experience at the neonatal unit, that Tyler, though tiny, was certainly not among the smallest. Some were close to a pound. Many had few or no visitors in the intensive care unit. The staff, unfortunately accustomed to this, would seek volunteers to come and hold, cuddle and play with those infants who had little contact otherwise. How could it be that they were brought into this world and then ignored?

I was able to finally see our Tyler five days later when I was dismissed and could travel to the Rockford NICU unit. I thought he was the most beautiful sight in the world. He had lovely dark hair, and tiny hands and feet. I couldn't wait for him to come back to Freeport and then home.

Tyler returned to Freeport on April 1st. I would go to see him several times and attempt to breast feed him, but he was just too small. I longed to have him at home. On April 13th, Steve's birthday, it was 70 degrees. The sun was shining when Tyler came home. I had my family at home together - life was indeed good.

The first couple of years of Tyler's life were stressful, however. He was extremely susceptible to respiratory infections and pneumonia, and was hospitalized five or six times. Other difficulties with eating, crawling and walking were encountered. It was also determined that due to Tyler's continuing small size that he most closely resembled having a condition known as Russle-Silver Syndrome, characterized by short stature, fine features along with an unexplained small birth weight. Tyler was again subject to more medical intervention in the form of growth hormone shots.

We tried to give him his injections after his bath at night, so he could go to sleep afterward. But he quickly caught on to the routine. Tyler would have to be held while mom would give his leg a poke. He often turned to 4 year old Ben to be held and comforted. It was not a happy time for Tyler.

As the years have quickly gone by, we have continued to be amazed and delighted with Tyler's progress. He has overcome many obstacles and is now an excellent student. Still small, he throws a mean football pass, plays soccer well, and cannot wait to play junior tackle. He enjoys all the usual electronic games and rough housing with Ben and friends. He is devoted to his cats and can't wait to have a dog someday.

Tyler and Ben are the best of friends. Ben is still protective of Tyler, though they also have a typical sibling relationship.

We have been blessed and are forever grateful for what has been offered to our family, Sarah, Ben and one small miracle named Tyler. Thank you for these gifts.

Vicki Spyrison

4

Quiet Heroes

A hero is someone who has given his or her life to something bigger than oneself.

Joseph Campbell

A thousand words will not leave so deep an impression as one deed.

Henrik Ibsen

Making a Difference
Freeport teen visits every patient in hospital

Her nickname is "Sunshine" and it is easy to see how she got it.

Leah Mendelsohn, 19, of Freeport, beamed her sunshine and good cheer into the rooms of about 75 patients Saturday in Freeport Memorial Hospital as she set off on her self-appointed mission to make a difference in their lives.

Mendelsohn's project was part of the national Make A Difference Day campaign where people volunteer their time to help wherever and however they can. She came up with the idea to visit every patient in the hospital on her own, and then spent about 20 hours coordinating and completing her task.

She said she began her rounds at 1 p.m. Saturday and finished about 6:30 p.m. She left behind a trail of smiles, laughter and some puzzled looks as well.

"The majority of patients couldn't believe that someone would visit them for no reason. They were just so happy and very supportive of me," Mendelsohn said.

Her visits had a powerful impact on a few of the patients.

"They all were really happy, and some were even moved to tears," she said.

One such grateful patient was Alice Adams of Freeport who met up with an old friend who was visiting down the hall, and made a new friend when Mendelsohn knocked on her door.

"I think it's wonderful. It's lovely and I appreciate the gifts. She's a very good one and I enjoyed it," Adams said.

Adams, along with the other patients, received a care package of flowers, pens and pencils, stickers, magnets and a balloon. Mendelsohn also gave out letter openers, some ceramic mugs and T-shirts to the kids in the pediatric unit. All of the supplies were donated by local merchants whom Mendelsohn contacted for her project.

"I never thought I would get this much support," she said.

While deciding to visit every patient in the hospital may seem like an ambitious project, it is typical Leah, according to her mother Roxanne Goodman who accompanied her daughter for awhile Saturday.

"She's a very special kid. She's always giving of herself to make a difference in someone's life or day," Goodman said.

Leah volunteers her time for the Friends Forever Humane Society, Wildlife Inc., refereeing soccer, Camp Success and the American Red Cross.

As if that schedule is not busy enough she also juggles a full-time job and a full course load at Highland Community College just for good measure. She carries a 3.5 GPA studying special education, according to Goodman.

Mendelsohn said she got the idea for the hospital visits from a magazine article on Make A Difference Day. She then spoke with Nancy Eckert of the Volunteer Services department at the hospital, who also embraced the idea.

Though she did most of the work on the project herself, Mendelsohn did enlist the help of students from Taylor Park and Blackhawk Elementary Schools who made get-well cards for the patients. Mendelsohn made sure each person she visited got a card.

Each participant who completes a project for the Make A Difference Day campaign now has the opportunity to write an essay on what he or she did and submit it to the national campaign coordinators. A donation will be made in the participant's name to a favorite charity.

The announcement of the winners will not come until January.

Although many of the patients were the recipients in Mendelsohn's project, she took away something from the day as well, and that was a feeling she was helping to bring some happiness to a few people who otherwise may not have an occasion to smile.

"Some of them had no one that would come visit them. I like to help people because it makes me feel good," she said.

Todd McKenna

Help!

It was not enough that we had suffered the worst winter weather in almost a century. It was April 5th. Spring had arrived; crocuses, daffodils, hyacinths, and early tulips were lined up in neat rows awaiting their signal to bloom. But the winter we thought was gone executed another vengeful attack. At mid-morning, the snow began in earnest. A biting north wind drove the large swirling snowflakes savagely past the windows, obliterating the whole outdoors. Finally, exhausting all of its fury, the storm relented, leaving high snowdrifts and clogged roads in its wake.

The next morning, the snow lay tranquil in a 14-inch blanket of glistening white on my driveway and sidewalk. I worried how I could remove all that snow without the help of my faithful handyman who was ill. Then the snowplow made its appointed rounds and added insult to injury. The huge snowdrifts were rearranged from the street onto my driveway exit. Now, a three-and-a-half foot wall existed between me and the street. I was trapped in my own garage, twenty miles and two hours from a long-awaited appointment with my dentist.

Snowfall of lesser proportion had brought any number of snow shoveling applicants to my door. Today, none came. With reluctance, I prepared for the job necessity had forced upon me. Dressed warmly and armed with snow shovel and broom, I began removing the thick white blanket. Little by little, I pushed the snow to the driveway's edge, lifting it only if I had to. I transferred it to the bank that was beginning to build along the edge.

Each shovelful got heavier as the bank grew higher. I vowed this snow was half cement as I felt a wave of heat surge over me. I opened my coat; off came my hat and scarf. A little discomfort never hurt anyone, I told myself as I continued shoveling. Soon I felt a trickle of perspiration on my brow. It was time for another layer to go. I should have worn my sweatsuit to begin with, I thought, as I began to perspire freely, despite my efforts at cooling off. But the job was not nearly done, and as much as I hated to admit it, my poorly toned muscles were showing the strain. Snow shoveling was hard work. Why did it look so easy when someone else was doing it?

The sun's emergence at mid-morning warmed the cold air and brought others out to clear their walk. I was heartened when three boys came to shovel the walks across the street. Perhaps they would consider taking another job when they finished there? In the meantime, scraping shovels and the whir of snowblower motors resounding through the crisp air of the misplaced winter day urged me on. After all, weren't we all in this together? Why should I just feel sorry for me?

I finally reached the place on the drive where the churned-up snow from the street formed a wall. I vowed this snow is all cement. I complained to myself. Stopping to rest, I noticed with dismay the three boys across the street were gone. They escaped without my notice and with them my only prospect for help. Feeling tired and abandoned, I was roused from my state of gloom by a voice behind me saying, "Could you use a little help?" I turned quickly to find a smiling neighbor standing ready with his snowblower. "You bet I could," was my eager reply.

Operator and snowblower made quick work of all the snow on the long walk around my corner lot and the wall that hemmed me in. "I have the best neighbors in the world," I gratefully acknowledged to my benefactors, as we sat over a cup of coffee later that morning.

As I watched my considerate neighbor guide his snowblower home, I reflected. It's the good things like this in life that count; the unexpected, thoughtful deed and a willing hand that helps in time of need.

Ruth P. Fleming

Rescue

I swam toward the beach with long strokes, the same measured, full breast-stroke which had won me a couple of trophies back in Illinois, in Read Park Pool. Other bathers stayed much closer to the shore, I watched them carousing, throwing beach balls to each other, closing in on the other bathers. In spite of strong strokes I wasn't making headway toward the beach. I vaguely remembered something I had heard in Physics class about the tides: Twice a day they went out, this must be the period of the outgoing tide.

I changed my stroking, took the more powerful, shorter whacks that I used at the end of my laps in Read Park. Swimming in that manner I shortened the distance between me and the beach, yet I remained far off the shore and in deep water. Suddenly I floated into a zone where the oncoming ocean broke into white-caps. The waves took me unaware, crashing over my head. I swallowed water, sickening sea water that tasted of foul seaweed and fuel oil. I gulped it in big swallows.

My burst of energy was tiring, the muscles of my arms and thighs ached. I turned over for the more relaxing backstroke, a stroke which also allowed me to spot the approaching waves and let me prepare for their onslaught. Even though I would barely make headway against the tide that way, I could rest and resume my breaststroke approach later. Breakers or not, I soon had to turn forward to start anew my sally toward dry land.

Crashing waves broke over my head again and began to pull my entire body with them. I glimpsed death. I rolled in the water, often completely immersed. Some waves pulled me down far enough for my feet or hands to touch bottom, letting fine sand trickle through my toes and fingers. The times when I was submerged became longer, I couldn't hold my breath that long and belted lots more water. My tired arms flailed the surface uselessly against the mighty Atlantic Ocean. I felt no pain and, rather than swimming, began to dream:

This fling in the Atlantic started with a vacation at Aunt Lulu's house. Aunt Lulu's real name was Louise. She and her family lived on Long Island at the fringe of New

York City. It was my first time at any seaside location and, expert swimmer whom I though myself to be, I begged my hosts to take me to a beach. Finally, on this oppressively hot Sunday, my cousin Randy and I took off for John's Beach State Park. Randy knew the way: A city bus to a railroad station, then an overcrowded sweltering train to another bus ride for the beach. Heat waves shimmered over sand and dune grass at the park. But the water seemed cool and looked very inviting. We waded in.

I soon left Randy behind. He was bookish while I considered myself an athlete.

"You swim ahead," he said. "meanwhile I'll unpack our lunch."

I, the landlubber, would show my seacoast cousin something about aquanautics. The sea water was easy to swim out in, and more thrilling than the streams, lakes and chlorinated pools I had swum in around the Midwest. Tossed about hopelessly in the sea twenty minutes after I had wetted my ankles in the cool waves — it seemed like an eternity — I dreamt on:

I didn't think of the future I would miss if I never set foot on dry land again: the Phi Beta Kappa student I would be, the famous lawyer I would become. Instead I saw my past through rose-colored lenses. I reflected on the prizes I had won in school sports events, I thought of my family and all the fascinating places we had driven to together: Mackinac Island, Estes Park, ski areas. I reflected on the friends I had made at various times, especially on Amanda, the cute girl I had taken to the prom and who had since become my steady.

I looked up through the blinding spray and became aware of three tall young men from far up on the beach who approached. They passed the other bathers and were closing in on me. When the water reached the neck of the point man he flung something overhead. A float attached to a line flew in my direction. It landed about ten feet in front of me. I paddled to it with my last strength and grabbed. My feet touched bottom after the lifeguards yanked the line a few times. Choking for breath and gasping I stumbled to the beach between my rescuers.

The lifeguards laid me head down near the water's edge. I saw my cousin, soon I also spied a large crowd surrounding us, no doubt hoping for my death. Then I couldn't see the lifeguards any longer. I spewed water for the longest time. When it let up Randy asked:

"How'd you feel? You think you can stand up on your feet?"

"I guess so."

"I suppose you've seen enough ocean beaches for a while. Let's head for home!"

"We can't do that yet, Randy. First I must go by the lifeguards to thank them for saving my life. Perhaps also to offer them something for their bravery. How much do you feel my life is worth?"

"You don't have to contribute anything, Matt. Saving lives is their job, they get paid for it."

"The pay can't be much. I know because the people of our Park District tried to hire me as a lifeguard before I decided to come out to New York. They talked about passes to the pool, the free uniforms we would get, the deep tans we would sport, the idolizing girls. Pay was never mentioned. In fact, saving lives wasn't mentioned either. Let's hustle over to the lifeguard tower."

"So you plan to give them what your life's worth, Matt?"

"My life is worth everything I own, including what my parents have already mailed in to Wadsworth College for tuition. But since I don't have all that dough on me I'll just give every penny in my pocket."

"And let me pay your fare back?"

"Okay, I'll hold on to carfare."

When we two youngsters reached the lifeguard station, I didn't recognize the boy sitting on top, or any of the others hanging around with the beach beauties at the bottom of the tower.

"Where are the guys who pulled me out of the drink?" I asked.

"Gone, buddy! We had a shift change ten minutes ago."

"You have their names?"

"Nope. So many guys work around here you can't know them all."

People from the city were still streaming to the park. Randy and I had an almost empty train for our homeward journey. Randy made me promise that I wouldn't tell his mother about my misadventure; he didn't want to be barred from future trips to the beaches. Then he was silent.

Since I wasn't allowed to express my gratitude to the lifeguards who had saved me, I resolved to pay for my rescue by always assisting persons in trouble, in danger, people who needed a helping hand. I have helped often whenever an occasion presented itself. I have also often thought of my rescuers through the following 50 years; yet, I still believe that something remains of the debt which I owe to the gallant lifeguards of John's Beach.

Ernst Wolff

The River

It doesn't seem so long ago, really. And yet indeed, it was sixty years ago. In those days I could run $2^1/_2$ miles, barefooted in the open desert, to my cousins' house along the river, and never pass a road or a house.

Nowadays, in Tucson, Arizona, a small shopping mall stands where the jerky was hung along our barbed wire fence to dry.

I was probably 8 or 9, that summer, when my cousins and I went to play in the sand of the bone dry Rillito River. Not like rivers around here, the water only rose after a hard rain or two. We could hear it roar a half mile away from our house. Sometimes. we went down just to see its raw power rushing by with all kinds of flotsam on its back, uprooted from its passage.

We didn't have television then and the radio was only on now and then in the evenings for the news. The Tucson Daily Star was an old format newspaper dating from the days of the Territory; so it didn't dwell much on natural phenomenon either.

At any rate, I just vaguely heard that there were such things as flash floods in the rains, but I only thought that applied after heavy, thunderstorms, if they happened at all.

My cousins and I often played in the sandy creek bottom because there you could run, jump, and play without being conscious of a possible rattler or other vermin that might be hidden for the coolness under a brush or rocks. On this sunny afternoon I began to hear a vague unfamiliar roar, distant but powerful. Looking to the east I could see it coming, --a solid sheet of water maybe a foot or so tall and behind that, maybe thirty yards riding on its top, another wall of water, and behind that another.

With the frontier training of a child, knowing to think and act fast, I decided the which-way-to-run that saved our lives. I had no idea how deep the river would run because the rain had fallen in the mountains far away. There was a small sand island with scrub bushes which would become the shallow side, and there was a mud cliff about twenty feet high cut on the curve where the river headed northward.

The cliff was farther, but the sand island may not, and indeed did not, stand above the torrent. None of us could swim, and anyway the edges of the layers were whirling as they came rattling bushes, wreckage, and rocks in a current we could not have survived.

In a split second of appraisal and judgment (probably helped by my trusty guardian angel), I rounded up the cousins, and made them run hell-bent for the cliff—no time for them to argue, "Why?" Aiming at a sort of crack in the mud cliff, a place we would never have tackled in the heat of the day, because of the likelihood of resting rattlers, coyotes, or even wildcats escaping the merciless summer sunshine, we scrambled up the steep slope pulling ourselves up by the scraggly bushes. I came up last, like any good herder, but cousin Bernice, when she felt the flood suck at her knees, froze in her tracks and wouldn't budge.

The water was already pulling at my wrist as it accelerated to make the curve, and one more layer of churning water would have swept us away.

I managed in desperation to claw right over her, and drag her up the ravine to safety, sputtering and resisting. We probably had 15 or 20 seconds to pull ourselves the rest of the way. Thank goodness the scraggly growth in its melting mud did not give way from our unexpected weight.

Looking back on those days, I doubt that we thought much about it, never told anyone, and probably resumed our play after resting. I didn't think of myself as heroic, but I then made up my mind to always watch and listen, and maybe try to figure out the "what-ifs" before, not after.

M. Joy Swingley

A Man Named Ward

There are many men who walk upon the face of this earth,
Many of whom don't truly realize their value or worth.

The man that I write about is humble and worth his weight in gold,
Whether it be his stories or the kindness he bestows.

This certain man whose name happens to be Ward,
Rules with gentleness and by the word of the Lord.

He bestows upon his flock, his wisdom, humor, and gentle ways,
By helping us remember that we're God's children on our darkest days.

He grins and bears the days when he has some pain,
But his love of the Lord our God is never, never in vain.

We wish him many years of happiness and good health,
His true commitment to God will give him heavenly wealth.

We hope he will be with us for many, many years,
To help through all the joys and even the tears.

He makes us laugh and then to smile,
He always is there to walk with you the extra mile.

Ward, you are truly a blessing sent from heaven above,
We care for, wish the best for, but mostly send you our love.

Many thanks for all you have done to make us all feel so very blessed.

Vicky Busker

Even if it's a little thing, do something for those who have need of help, something for which you get no pay but the privilege of doing it.

Albert Schweitzer

My Aunt Ruth

My aunt, Ruth Hiatt, is a very remarkable lady.

She has spent most of her life in service to others. As a Nazarine minister's wife, she was a helpmate to him in various capacities such as playing the piano for the services, accompanying him to visit those in hospitals and shut-ins and teaching Sunday School.

After becoming a widow in 1964, she continued to play piano for her church as well as the monthly services at the Willow Apartments where she resides. She would sit with older folks enabling them to remain in their own homes as well as tended to children from time to time.

But, the most remarkable thing about her is that this year 1997, turning 97 years old, she occupies her time 5 days a week making surgical drapes, exam table sheets, surgeons' caps & masks, sterilizing wrappers and all types of drapes needed to perform surgery. All these items she makes out of bed sheets.

On May 1, 1990, her nephew, Victor Binkley, a surgeon and medical director in Haiti near Port-A-Prince asked her if she would be interested in making exam table covers for him to use in the mission field. He brought her the first 8 sheets and it has expanded to include all other items mentioned above.

This year it has been estimated to be over 800 items that she alone has made for the mission field.

She looks forward to each new day setting goals of what she hopes to accomplish for that day.

Although physically she is slowing down, her mind, hands, and generous spirit continue to be a blessing to others. She vows to continue making these supplies as long as the need is there and she is able.

Colleen Dornink

'Happening'

Roger Hill's 'Happening': A Story of Inspiration for Others
This Freeport artist calls it "a miracle and a quick answer to my prayer."

"When I was in deep trouble and called on God for help, he heard me."
Roger says it was September 1.

He was chatting with a neighbor on his cordless phone. She told him it was sure raining at her place. With that piece of news, they finished their conversation. In his wheelchair, he headed for the ramp leading up to his house.

"The rain let loose and I had to back in the house up a slippery ramp. My feet began to slip. They pushed off the ramp and I landed in the bushes with both my arms under the chair. It was raining cats and dogs," said Roger.

He realized that there was no use to call for help. He could not be heard.

The rain was running into his shoes, and he lay there helpless.

"To top it all off, my chair was laying on top of a dead gopher, and the cats were hiding in the flower bed," said Roger.

"Then I said to God, I am in deep trouble. You have to help me."

Just about that time a car drove in. Roger hollered. The man jumped out of the car, moved the wheelchair off of Roger, grabbed Roger and took him into the house.

As it turned out, Roger knew that this guy was the world wrestling champ in his class. "I said, 'Thank you God, when you send help you send the best.' This guy handled me like a kid, and I weigh 225 pounds."

Arriving at that helpful moment were Roger's niece, Rachel, and her new husband, Jim Gruenwald.

They had just stopped by to say "Hello" en route home from their honeymoon trip.

After Roger dried off, Rachel brought out her $10,000 violin and treated him to celestial music.

"If you don't believe in the power of prayer, just ask me," said Roger. "I can tell you differently, 'cause I know."

Olga Gize Carlile

Duane Smith

His Answer

It happened during one of those sweltering summers that boasted of muggy days and tornadoes. Although I was already 10 years old, frequent tornadoes in the area kept me so frightened that I daily searched the skies for questionable-looking clouds and tried to identify those which might announce the approach of a tornado. Then we would have time to take refuge in the storm cellar near the house.

One evening the air seemed unusually oppressive and I thought I could sense a tornado on the way. Yet in spite of huge mounds of black clouds piling up in the west my two older sisters were allowed to attend a party near-by. Sixteen year-old Audrey picked them up and they were off in an old Model T car.

I can still remember how I sat on the front steps after they left, watched the fireflies and tried to keep from worrying about the distant rumble of thunder and the constant flash of heat lightning.

Our whole family was greatly relieved when Audrey brought my sister home early and because of the approaching storm, she was on the way to her home in a matter of seconds. We were glad that she had only two miles to go.

By this time the thunder seemed closer and jagged streaks of lightning carved the inky blackness of the sky. I kept my vigil and listened intently to the hollow silence that followed each clap of thunder. Then I heard it——-The low terrible roar of the wind!

" It's a tornado! " I screamed. "We have to go to the cellar!" But it was already too late. The wind struck and everyone scattered to close windows and doors. The rain and hail came and with every blast of the wind the house quivered. We held pillows against the windows to keep them from shattering. I was certain that the wind would blow us away and we would all be killed. However, the minutes passed and we were still safe.

As the immediate danger subsided, my father's concern was for Audrey, the young girl, alone on a country road with a tornado following in her path. The car was probably swept off the road and who could say what had happened to her? Telephone wires were down and there was no way we could know.

But my father put his doubt into action. He struggled through the wind and rain, bridled a faithful work-horse, jumped on her back and was immediately swallowed up in the storm, as he set out in search of the girl.

As time passed the wind diminished to some extent, but the rain continued in torrents. Now my mother, my sisters and I silently huddled around the kitchen table in the pale glow of the kerosene lamp. Hoping and praying that Dad would be safe.

After what seemed to be hours of waiting, there came a sloshing sound on the porch and Dad burst in almost like the storm itself.

"She's safe! She's safe!" he cried breathlessly. Somehow Audrey had reached home just as the storm broke.

And so it happened that one night long ago my father demonstrated his answer to the age-old question, "Am I my brother's keeper?"

Vera Emmert Johansen

A teacher affects eternity; he can never tell when his influence stops.

Henry Adams

Nothing Against Motherhood

This is about a letter that was written recently but happened many years ago. At that time I was principal of Freeport High School. Part of the letter follows.

"Dear Mr. Baumgartner: Some letters are a long time in the thinking stage and finally get written. Consider this one of these letters.

About 27 years ago to this day I was a young married woman with one year of college to finish. Having graduated from Freeport High School in 1960, I was then scheduled to do my student teaching there in the fall of 1963. However, I became pregnant and things being as they were then, just assumed that I would not be able to continue my schooling.

I came to you and told you that I would not be doing my student teaching and that I planned to drop out of college and not finish my senior year. While I am sure these were not your exact words, you said something like, 'We have nothing against motherhood at this school. If you drop out now you will never return to finish. We will still be glad to have you come to student teach at Freeport High School.'

I can't tell you how this vote of confidence and encouragement affected my life. I did do my student teaching with Jeanette Lloyd (at Freeport High School) and did graduate from Northern Illinois University. I went on to receive my M.S. degree in guidance and counseling.

I have often told them the story about you. I was a very average student but you took the time to encourage me and say, "You can do it." Words can never express my gratitude and appreciation."

She concludes with, "Oh, yes, and what happened to that little baby born in the spring of 1964? What else? He's a high school teacher working and trying hard to make a difference in the lives of students. I shall be forever grateful. Darlene Hughes Axtell."

The above letter was written by Darlene Hughes Axtell. She is now Director of the Guidance Program in Appleton, Wisconsin.

She goes on to say that she does a great deal of staff development. One course she teaches is the "The Skillful Teacher" in which there is a discussion of "the difference teachers make in the lives of students."

Reuben Baumgartner

True happiness...is not attained through self-gratification, but through fidelity to a worthy cause.

Samuel Johnson

One Person's Global Reachout

Freeport's Kerrylyn Whalen validates the maxim, "One person can make a difference." If a psychic had told her in July, 1992, that she'd soon quit her job as a pharmacist and liquidate her assets to live in the Amazon Rain Forest, she wouldn't have believed it. But that's just what happened.

This unlikely chain of events was triggered by a friend's invitation to go on a trip to the Peruvian jungle. There, they would observe the exotic birds and plants. It sounded fun and adventurous, so Kerrylyn went along.

Since she was not an experienced camper, the rigors of survival in a primitive venue without running water seemed overwhelming. Plus all the required vaccinations! Her Third World awareness was based on PBS documentaries and some articles she'd read in the *National Geographic*. Another drawback was not being able to speak Spanish.

Kerrylyn found that living in the jungle has daily challenges, like locating potable drinking water, finding a place to go to the bathroom, and discovering ways to ward off invasions by snakes, scorpions, tarantulas, and monster mosquitoes. Diarrhea and stomach upsets plague the natives and visitors alike.

On the positive side, Kerrylyn's first visit to the rain forest yielded many good experiences. She saw the sense of community and family values in the jungle village of Puerto Miguel. She shared her first aid kit and over-the-counter medicines, such as aspirin and Pepto Bismol, to help a dozen villagers and some tourists. The villagers had nothing to relieve even minor health problems. The nearest town with electricity, telephones and a hospital is a day-and-a-half journey via canoe. And even if these people could go to the hospital, in most cases they had no money to pay.

Kerrylyn's experiences on that first visit made her want to return. Only this time, she was determined to bring as much medicine as possible to help the rain forest people.

In 1993, she established an emergency medical outpost, stocked with pharmaceuticals most of us in the United States take for granted. They're all readily available from our nearby drug store, including toothbrushes and other oral hygiene aids.

Kerrylyn has returned every year since for prolonged stays to stock and service her jungle clinic. It has become a lifetime commitment. Medical supplies are furnished from funds donated by church groups and friends. Today it serves about 1,800 people who live in nine villages on the Yarapa River near the headwaters of the Amazon. She can now speak Spanish and has linked up with doctors, hospitals, the Peruvian government, and international service organizations to join in her quest.

She's become aware of indigenous health problems, such as carnasidad, a disease which causes growths in the eyes. These growths can cause blindness when exposed to the equatorial sun. Wearing baseball caps helps alleviate the problem. So Kerrylyn accepts donations of baseball caps for the children to wear.

When Kerrylyn ran out of money in the spring of 1995, she returned to the United States and settled in Freeport to head Shopko's pharmacy. The emergency station is still operating with the help of several villagers whom she taught basic first aid and coordination by her husband, Roy Rodriguiz, a Puerto Miguel native she met after moving to Peru. She visits there about four times a year, each time bringing more supplies and allowing her husband to spend more time with their daughters, two-year-old Elysia and six-month-old Katelyn.

Here are some of Kerrylyn's observations based on her rain forest experiences: "People are the same in many ways, yet they vary in their expectations in life. Thus, if you don't expect a lot, you tend to appreciate what you have.

If we're going to live in a "world society," we must respect people. In Puerto Miguel, the people don't have anything. They wanted to give me something, so they would give me food. Oftimes they would give the only food they had for the day. I couldn't say no because that would hurt their pride. And their pride is more important than their hunger. I couldn't eat it because I felt guilty, so I'd give it to somebody else who was hungry. Wouldn't it be great if people would live the Golden Rule rather than just talk about it?'

"Help people any way you can. Mow your neighbor's yard, watch their kids, go to the grocery store for them, etc. Do unselfish things. By being unselfish, in a way you are selfish because there's nothing more rewarding than taking time to help somebody else."

Kerrylyn spent her childhood in LaSalle, Illinois and later lived in Chicago and Montana. She finished a five-year pharmaceutical degree in three years by the age of twenty. At twenty-three, she had paid off her student loan and bought her first house and a car. Later, she successfully passed the bar, having gone to law school full-time while working as a pharmacist forty-five hours a week. She received a Masters Degree in Health Law from Loyola. Kerrylyn lives in Freeport. Between the periodic treks to Peru, you'll find her in the pharmacy of the local Shopko store.

Dick Shouer

5

Overcoming Adversity

Adversity is the first path to Truth.

Byron

We can't form children on our own concepts; we must take them and love them as God gives them to us.

Johann von Goethe

God's Gift

How old are you, Claire?

"Two."

No. How old are you Claire?

"Three."

No-o. How old are you, Claire?

"Four."

YES! That's it. You're four years old.

We have been asking Claire that question since she was old enough to talk. She has always asserted that she is two as a first response. Why does she do this, we wonder?

Claire had her first seizure one month after her second birthday. We didn't know what it was at the time. A warm, moist bathroom with the shower running and holding her gently, she eventually regained her normal state of awareness after spitting up. We thought at the time that she had been suffering from a cold and just couldn't breathe well for a while. That was the case until the Memorial Day weekend. At about 2 a.m. on Saturday, Claire started to lose consciousness. Then she started a weird chewing motion, eventually we could tell that she was having a seizure. I called a friend, who is a family practitioner. His advice was to take her to the emergency room. She received Valium and Dilantin, an anti-seizure medicine, through an IV and came out of the seizure within a hour. The nightmare was just beginning.

We were referred to a pediatric neurologist for Claire and began the arduous and trying process of trying to determine what was causing the seizures. We prayed that it wasn't a tumor. We prayed that it was only transient, maybe caused by a virus. Was it epilepsy? We had no idea of what was to come. Claire underwent the usual work-up of an EEG, CT scan and MRI. Blood samples were drawn and more tests were ordered.

"Daddy!"

I'm sorry, Claire.

"No, daddy, no!"

We have to do this, Claire. We have to find out what's wrong.

"Daaaddddyyy!"

The first doctor couldn't find the right spot to draw the fluid out of her spinal column. Claire writhed and cried. Her pediatric neurologist then steadied his hand and swiftly inserted the needle between the spinal lamina and withdrew an ample amount of cerebral spinal fluid. The doctors and staff sighed in relief. I held Claire close to me and tried to soothe her. She was weeping and shaking. Her hair was wet from tears, hers and mine. What else was she going to have to go through? I carried her back to her mother who nursed her to sleep. I melted onto the bed, spent from physical and mental exhaustion. We still didn't have an answer, but we heard the word "leukodystrophy" for the first time. We looked it up in the pediatric neurology book.

Then we broke down and cried. The future was not very promising. Mary and Veronica tried to console us. Their childhood shouldn't be about pain and suffering for their sister. It should be about joy and laughter. Playing with their sister, not dreading the next seizure. They didn't fully understand. How could they? We didn't understand it ourselves.

"I don't want to throw up!"

It's okay, Claire. Mommy and Daddy are here.

Claire gagged again and looked to us for some form of comfort. We held her tightly and prayed. We had learned what an aura is. It is like a premonition of a forthcoming seizure. Claire's was primarily a pronounced gag reflex. As she would become older she began to recognize these symptoms and be fearful of another seizure. She had seven more that summer and eventually another in December, four days before Christmas, while I was in Michigan attending my uncle's funeral. Irena had prayed that day that I would come home earlier than my scheduled flight at seven p.m. Her message must have reached me, as I took the four o'clock flight to Rockford and was home by seven.

We had finally taken Claire to Children's Memorial Hospital in Chicago in September of 1995, seven months after her first episode and three months after most of her tests were done. We still didn't have a definitive diagnosis. We knew that the EEG was abnormal. We knew that there was increased white matter in the brain from the MRI results. We knew that she was allergic to Tegretol, another anti-seizure medication, that was tried initially. What we didn't know was what was causing the seizures. Dr. Charles Swisher at Children's Memorial Hospital was like the kindly uncle we remember from our childhood. This gentle, unassuming physician broke the news gently. He had consulted with the radiologist and some of the leading experts in the world about Claire. The diagnosis was unclassified leukodystrophy, a chronic degenerative condition affecting the central nervous system, especially increasing the white matter in the brain. The long-term prognosis was not good. Most children only live an average of three to five years after the diagnosis. Dr. Swisher gave us the number of the United Leukodystophy Foundation in Sycamore, Illinois. He told us about their second opinion program. Maybe there was a different diagnosis or something more specific.

"Mommy!Mommmmyyy!"

Claire wasn't feeling well. She was starting to gag again. This was the morning after our meeting with Dr. Swisher. We had spent the night at a friend's house in Chicago and now Claire was starting to get sick again. We gave her the Valium we had been prescribed to give when a seizure starts. It wasn't helping. We tried reaching Dr. Swisher. No luck. Finally, I reached one of his residents.

"Bring her to the hospital," he said.

Do we need an ambulance?

"Just try to get here as soon as you can," he replied.

It took us forty minutes to get there. She had been seizing for almost two hours non-stop. We finally arrived at the emergency room. The seizure had stopped five minutes before arriving. We carried an exhausted, sleeping child into the hospital. We filled her first prescription for Neurontin, a new anti-seizure medicine. It had a great track record in Europe, but had just been used in the States for the past two to three years.

The Neurontin has been very successful in minimizing her symptoms. Claire has only had two seizures since December, 1995. God's blessings were many during 1996 when Claire was free of seizures. Irena was pregnant during the last nine months of the year. I attended my first United Leukodystrophy Foundation Conference in July and was impressed and moved by the parents who had lost children to this unremitting disease. They had come to offer love and support to those parents that were experiencing what they had been through. The physicians and researchers were some of the most dedicated and compassionate people that I have had the pleasure of meeting. The sight of them sitting on lawn chairs and reading MRIs by the light of the setting sun while answering each parent's questions will linger in my mind for a long time.

Teresa was born on January 1, 1997 at six in the morning. Claire was a big sister. She had shared in the blessed event. She woke an hour before the birth and joined the family for Teresa's arrival at home. What a joyous way to ring in the New Year!

How old are you, Claire?

"Four."

When will you be five?

"I have Barney birthday."

I know, Claire, but when is your birthday?

"January."

January, what?

"January Fifth."

Good job, Claire. Good job!

"I have a Barney birthday!"

Right. You'll have a Barney Birthday.

We get caught up in our daily lives. Claire makes sure we know she is there. Sometimes the stares from people who think she is just misbehaving are difficult to deal with. The brain damage that has occurred may be permanent with developmental delays already apparent. We work with her daily and overall she has shown signs of improvement, She can be such a happy child and is truly loving toward others. The outbursts and occasional violent behavior seem to stem from frustration at being unable to fully communicate to others. Claire's neurologist is encouraged by the physical and mental progress she has made. We thank God for each day that she is with us.

"Daddy's home"

Hi, Claire. Give daddy a hug, big girl.

"I love you, daddy."

I love you too, Claire.

None of us knows what the future holds. We try to do the best we can as parents, as spouses, as people. We often find ourselves in need of the love, support and kindness of family, friends, health care providers, and strangers. When our child's well-being is at stake, we do whatever is in our power to try to improve the health of our child. Claire is no exception. We have tried every form of therapy and alternative care we are aware of in order to help her. We cling to any signs of improvement, while wondering what the day will bring. Ultimately, we put our lives and Claire's life in God's hands. Light a candle. Say a prayer. Ask God's forgiveness. My first thought when Claire was diagnosed was that I may not see my little girl get married. I had always envisioned walking her down the aisle. The proud father sharing a special moment with his beloved daughter. Now I realize that I have offered her hand to someone most special, to the one who loves us most, to be a child of God.

Ready for bed, Claire.

"Read me a story, Daddy."

Which one, sweetheart?

"Owl Babies."

Once there were three baby owls. Sarah, and Percy and Bill. They lived in a hole in the trunk of a tree with their owl mother... Good night, Claire. Daddy loves you.

"I love you too, Daddy."

Sweet dreams, my love. Sweet dreams.

Roland Tolliver

Reflection

The word "brave" is bandied about too loosely these days. Simply playing the cards life deals, for example, isn't brave; it's merely prudent. Real bravery requires the presence of an option: the option of playing it safe, or putting everything at risk for someone else. I haven't known many who fulfilled that requirement. Just one person, actually —a frail, but grand old matriarch of 94.

I'll never forget the first time I met her: As I opened the screen door and stepped into the living room of her home, there she was. Surgery many years before had frozen her hip so that now she was forced to sit slouched in her lift-chair, looking small and frail, while at the same time, undeniably regal. Her face, furrowed by time, but softened by a still generous halo of silver hair, refused to acknowledge her 94 years, and eyes, more gray than the blue they once were, twinkled as they met mine. She didn't rise from her chair; but merely smiled in a warm, and disarming way, slowly extended her hand, and softly spoke my name—as though she'd been expecting me a long time and here I was at last.

I would soon discover that, usually, she sat in a second lift-chair in her den, surrounded by her library, family pictures, and mementos from her fascinating past. She made the arduous journey to that chair from her bed in the next room every morning after her day-lady came, and she pretty much stayed there until her night-lady arrived to make her dinner and put her to bed. At her feet, in her lap, or under her chair was Jingles, a small shaggy dog of dubious parentage, and equally doubtful character.

In between the departure of the day-lady and the arrival of the evening-lady, she sat positioned with a view of the window and enjoyed watching her hovering too near for innocent intent. When she tired of that, she might pick up her knitting needles, or a book, or a pen and stationery. Occasionally, she entertained a few friends who had keys to the house and would faithfully drop by to see her.

But at night, after her evening help had put her to bed and left, she was entirely alone. "Aren't you the least bit afraid?" friends and family would query; "Certainly not," she would reply, adding with a grin, "I'm a tough old bird, and

I'm perfectly safe...and perfectly happy."

In the years since her husband's death, and her incapacitation, she had relied heavily on her adored and adoring sons, and their daily visits, but she especially counted on her eldest who wasn't married. Often, sometimes four or five times a week, he would take her for long rides in the country. During these rides, he'd purposely ply her with questions which evoked happy memories. On Sundays, she could depend on his stopping by to take her to church, no easy task for either of them. Later, they'd stop for lunch, usually at a drive-in so that she wouldn't have to struggle getting in and out of the car. The mother of three sons myself, I know what these times must have meant to her.

Given her frailty, and the amount of time and attention a single son could devote to her, it was always a marvel to me that she had long been an advocate of his re-marriage. I'm sure she knew quite well that things were bound to change if he took a new wife. A wife would inevitably stake her claim on his time; and that would mean that he had less for her. She must have known that the rides wouldn't be as frequent, that she would seldom have him all to herself again. That her protracted solitude would have fewer intervals of respite. And yet strangely, one could almost see her sigh with relief when he did remarry.

She lived another five years after that marriage took place—and, during that time, she never once complained that she was getting less attention. She's been gone almost a year now, and we all miss her a great deal, especially I—the new daughter-in-law she bravely welcomed into her life.

Mary Doak Lockwood (copyright)

Why?

Early one morning the telephone rang and the caller was the principal of our local junior high school asking if I was free to substitute for a teacher who was ill that day. Since I had no other teaching assignment for the day, I agreed to accept the responsibility even though it was a difficult one. It involved a class of students who were disruptive, defiant and unwilling to learn. Suddenly I was frightened. Only last week a student had drawn a gun and fired at a teacher in this same school. How could I ever teach a whole class of young people who were known to be so difficult?

This question continued to haunt me as I ate breakfast and read our daily devotional guide. The scripture was taken from Isaiah 30:15, "In quietness and confidence shall be your strength." My fear vanished. From that moment and on through the day, God's words sustained me. I put my trust in Him knowing that He would guide and help me.

It wasn't easy, but in spite of the many trying situations I continued to speak quietly and kindly to each student during the day. I listened to their tirades and felt compassion for these children who evidently longed for love and understanding. I believe they sensed my caring and when they discovered that their rough language and ill-tempered ways were not upsetting me, they became more cooperative. It was a good day for all of us and I was pleased with their progress.

As I drove home that afternoon I said to myself, "I want to re-read that morning devotional because I can't remember anything but the scripture." So the first thing I did when I arrived home was to get the guide and turn to the day's reading. To my surprise the scripture was entirely different from what I had read in the morning and although I searched carefully, I finally had to give up. I couldn't find it.

The days passed by and the strangeness of the circumstances puzzled me but I was truly thankful for God's guidance that day.

One month later there was another telephone call for me to substitute for the same teacher and I accepted. I had no fear as I had previously. Before leaving for school I turned to the page in the devotional book for that day's reading and there in front of my eyes were the words I had been unable to locate a month earlier. In my haste that morning I had skipped a whole month's reading!

God works in wonderful ways to teach His children. How thankful I am!

Vera Emmert Johansen

The happiest people are those who are too busy to notice whether they are or not.

William Feather

Abundant Life... After Cancer

W hen the diagnosis is cancer, life becomes such a precious commodity. Things that we thought were so important before are now seen in a much different light. My healing process after breast cancer involved a deep faith in God, a supportive husband, family, and positive attitude. What helped me the most in my early battle was to keep myself occupied with helping others, not focusing just on myself.

I decided to open my own real estate office in 1975. I had achieved lifetime membership in the State Million Dollar Club working for several other real estate brokers. My two sons were grown by that time and were living out of state. I had several years experience in real estate and had established myself in land development and new home construction with my husband, Harold, a builder of custom homes. My own real estate company was something that I had wanted to do for a long time and I wasn't getting any younger. We bought a former grocery store on West Street, remodeled it, and my "dream" was born. Five years later I was told that I had breast cancer and would need surgery. I was so consumed with my business and my life that I did not have time for any "pity-parties!" I was in a service business that required full attention to my clients and to the brokers who worked for me. We enjoyed nine wonderful years, which passed quickly. I decided then to sell the building to an insurance agency and return to work for another broker. My "dream" business had served me well and it was time to move on. Life is an endurance run at best, but Christians never have to run the race alone.

My cancer experience was ultimately a "blessing in disguise," as it taught me many valuable lessons about myself and about other people as well. It opened the door for me to reach out to other women as a volunteer for the American Cancer Society's local 'Reach to Recovery' program. I truly experienced what was written in Romans 8:28, "all things work together for good to those who love God ." It has given me the opportunity to speak to women's groups about breast cancer. I often receive phone calls from anxious women who are awaiting surgery . It is always a joy to make a hospital call and reassure women that there is life after breast cancer. I encourage them to live every day with a positive attitude and happy outlook. I have had seventeen wonderful years since I was diagnosed, which could have been seventeen years of worry and fear for myself, my family and friends. We are not therapists, but we are trained as volunteers to be supportive people. We can offer hope, kindness, encouragement and empathy. We have "been there."

Retirement is not an option for my husband or myself, as long as our health permits. Most people look forward to retirement because they are unhappy with their jobs. We still feel that we can make a contribution in our businesses and in our community. Harold has had a couple of "delays" after suffering a heart attack and having four angioplasties. We have been in land development and new home construction for fifty years in Freeport and Stephenson County. Our labor, tears, sweat and pride are in well known areas from Carriage Hills to Royal Oaks and from Woodside Kort to recent developments in Springbrook and Oakwood Glyn. I have been a licensed realtor for the past thirty years. It has been exciting and rewarding to help people into their first homes and into their new homes. Now we are helping some of their children and grandchildren. The business has taken us full circle. We take pride in realizing that in our own small way we have helped Freeport grow. Harold had the pleasure and privilege of helping to construct the first *Habitat for Humanity* house in Freeport. I took part in establishing the Freeport Art Museum, which transformed an old school into what is now an art and cultural center. It is a valuable asset to Freeport and Stephenson County. Seven years ago several of us in the real estate profession started the *Needy Children's Christmas* project. Many of our local children and their parents have recieved toys, clothes and food baskets as a result of this collaborative effort. The joy on their faces makes me realize that the importance of giving to others makes our life much more fulfilling.

The first *Relay for Life* in Freeport was held in 1995. It was held at the Aquin High School track and was to raise funds for the American Cancer Society. I helped to establish a relay team, as I had many friends and connections from which to draw. Our enthusiastic team of eleven volunteers chose the appropriate name, "Survivors' Team." We had our team name printed on tee shirts and set off to collect as much money as we could for the Cancer Relay. Cancer survivors take the first lap of the day after the Color Guard marches in and the Star Spangled Banner is sung. Even rain and lightning (which forced us off the track for a while) were not enough to dampen the spirit of the teams and their mission. Our first place team raised $4400.00. The goal for the Relay was $5000.00, but a total of $12,200.00 was raised that first year.

The next year brought about twenty teams, a significant increase over the previous year. I was able to participate on the committee and help with planning for that year's event. Several corporate sponsors joined us, including the L.C. Ferguson Cancer Center, Today's Bank (now the Mercantile Bank) and The St. Paul Insurance Company, The Journal Standard and WFRL promoted the event. The highlight of that year's event for me was the evening Luminary Service. Candles were lit for those who have survived cancer and those who have lost the battle. Hundreds of candles illuminated the night from their places around the track and over the background of music the names of those whom the candles were purchased in honor or in memoriam of were read. The survivors talked and reflected on the day, the relay members and the community of friends, family and supporters sharing in the day's victory. We are planning for an even greater turnout this year . One of our teammates, who was taken at the young age of forty one, will be dearly missed from this year's relay. We plan on honoring her in a special memorial service. Life is often much too short.

I reflect back on one of the greatest highlights of my career, when I was selected as the "Realtor of the Year" by the Freeport Realtors in 1984. This was a rewarding, yet humbling honor. I went to a wonderful weekend celebration in Springfield, where I heard many people lament about how busy their lives are. I saw that then, as I do now. "That's good," I say. It keeps us from spending so much time worrying about our problems A woman's greatest concern with breast cancer is the fear it will return or spread. I remind them that we can go at anytime, don't waste that time with worry. Don't let your life be full of "what ifs" let it be full of "what can I do to help."

Each day is truly a gift from God! I firmly believe that He has a plan for each of our lives. Allow him to direct and instruct. He will do a much better job than we can. I always tell the women I meet, if your husband wants to go for a drive, forget the housework and go. If the children need your attention, give it. The benefits are tremendous! When those depressing days come along, and they do for all of us, call a friend and get together. See if someone has a special need in their life and help them. I guarantee that you will soon forget about what was so depressing. Sometimes when you ask someone how they are doing, they will reply, "pretty good, under the circumstances." I don't think you should ever be "under the circumstances", but "on top of them!" Happiness in our lives is a choice, so choose to be happy. It does make a difference and so can you. Make a difference in someone's life and you'll never regret it.

Now, if I can just master the computer, my life will be complete!

Peg Schoonhoven

A Shared Battle

Lydia Root knows what it's like to live under a sentence of death.

In 1986, following an operation to remove an ulcer, a test conducted on tissue samples from a section of her stomach showed conclusively that she had a deadly form of cancer, Adeno Carcinoma Linitus Plastica.

Her oncologist, a physician who specializes in the treatment of cancer, told her she had less than two years to live.

"And then he walks out of the room. No one tells you what you can do to make a difference in your recovery," the patient, Lydia Root said, "I felt like I was kicked by an elephant – hard."

About a dozen pictures of her husband, four sons, daughters-in-law and four grandchildren reside on a large piece of wall space in the living room of her ranch-style home. The words flow smoothly as she talks candidly about her condition, recovery and her mission to help others like herself who are willing to embrace life in an effort to keep their precious gift. Her soft, blue eyes don't reveal the inner strength she displayed at a time when many lose hope.

"I knew I would rather die trying to live than live waiting to die," she said.

Her immediate inspiration was author Norman Cousins' book "Anatomy of An Illness." When Cousins was faced with a potentially terminal illness, he left the hospital to get well," Root said.

She did the same. He took control of his environment and attitude. Root says when she arrived home from the hospital weakened from the surgery that took 40 percent of her stomach, and facing a year of chemotherapy, she did the same.

"I came home and asked my husband for control over the living room. I didn't watch or listen to the news for a year and played good music to help me relax, which boosts the immune system," she said.

A "committed Christian" - long before her illness, Root took great comfort in her faith and local faith community. The congregation at her home church, the Savannah Community United Church of Christ, were ready to do what they could to help. "They were very open and reached out to me in ways that they never had before. Their compassion was happily received," she says.

She asked three long-time friends who no longer live in northwest Illinois to write, call or drop a note to her whenever they could. Her husband and the rest of her family stood behind her decision to handle her own attempt at recovery. What Root did, although not necessarily by design, was create a healing team.

When she could eat after surgery, she avoided processed foods, sugar and empty calories, while eating fresh fruits and vegetables as well as other foods high in fiber and beta carotene. A former part-time physical education teacher, she knows exercise is an important part of feeling and being healthy. Though weakened considerably from her chemotherapy, she says she managed to walk about 2 miles almost every day. When the weather was poor, she went indoors and walked the long corridors of a local Methodist church.

Root learned self-hypnosis techniques to help her relax and reduce the ills caused by frequent chemotherapy treatments. She changed her attitude concerning putting drugs in her body, accepting the need for the chemotherapy to improve her chances of overcoming her cancer. "Learning self-hypnosis was the best thing I did for myself. It reduced or eliminated the side effects from the chemotherapy treatments. During the entire year I was undergoing chemotherapy, I never threw up," Root said with a hint of pride in her voice.

Still, several years after her original diagnosis, and already having beat the predictions of her doctors, she was weak and was a long way from returning to her previous lifestyle," I faced my mortality and I accepted being ready to die. But I was not ready to quit trying to recover," she said.

It wasn't until she gave her burden to God that her recovery began to speed up. "I was finally reminded who is really in control," Root said " I was looking at a sun-catcher on a window which read ' Let Go – Let God' It took a long time for me to let go and let God in and help me. I was trying to do it all myself... When I gave that up, I started getting well. I realized it wasn't all on my shoulders."

A nagging question Root could not get out of her mind was why no one had produced a videotape to help those who are diagnosed with a terminal ailment take charge of their own recovery. She says there were many excellent books and audiotapes, but not a video. "I felt other cancer patients needed to know what might help themselves."

A mini-cam was bought and a home produced tape was made. A copy of the tape fell into the hands of a cardiologist in St. Paul, Minn., who wanted to use the tapes in her medical practice. She thought Root needed to take the next step and produce professional-quality tapes and gave her $3,000 to help the project along.

Four years ago, KWQC-TV in Davenport donated the technical know-how, a camera crew and production manager to work on the project. Root says they began what was a slow, but rewarding process of producing the tapes, which Root wrote. Animals, cartoons and liberal doses of humor are featured in the tapes to make them less threatening and more enjoyable for people who are already under a great deal of stress.

"Many people contributed in this idealistic attempt to make the videos at a low cost. Two ministers, a priest, nutritionist, two therapeutic massage therapists and other area residents donated their time to make these videotapes," Root says.

The Anheuser Busch Clydesdales , the Lippizaner horses from northern Illinois and elephants from several circuses and the San Diego Wild Animal Park all help to teach people how to form and be a part of healing team, she says. The venture is not-for-profit. Once the production costs, which total about $20,000, are paid off, the profits will go toward the Cancer Awareness Group of Carroll County.

"I'm thrilled with the final product and I'm hearing good things from other cancer patients about them," Root said, with a smile coming to her face.

She is feeling much better and is looking forward to taking a trip to northern California to visit one of her sons. After defying the predictions of doctors and the odds of surviving her cancer, Root says the most important piece of advice she can give anyone who finds themselves in a similar position to hers is to "think positive."

"Kicked by An Elephant" details how to cope with being diagnosed with a terminal illness. "Hitch Up Your Healing Teams" gives information ranging from disease prevention to informing patients about resource material, stress reduction techniques and an extensive interview with Root detailing her winning her battle with cancer.

Gregory Douglas

Helplessness Supreme

I sit by my dying sister-in-law's bed,
and we talk of nothings, of everythings.
We walk thru the myths of ourselves to healings,
finishing unfinished business, clearing up foggy spots.

There is not much time now; she'll pass on soon.
New business to tend to; new places to explore; new life stories to create.

And I feel the urgency to finish this ending,
And I feel the drifting of her soul across the border to death.
And I feel the sadness of the family,
their unspoken cries of "Don't leave us yet ! We need more time! We need you!"

A lifetime of silence needing to be breached
before the chance is lost forever.
I feel their bewilderment, their confusion, their loss of control,
where control has always stood its stead before.

Helplessness supreme.

The inability to say, "I've loved you. You've meant so much to me."
And sharing "Remember when we's."

They do the death dance beside her bed.
Eyes downcast, feet shuffling, hands wringing
wanting to speak, guts <u>screaming</u> to speak,
but unable to utter the words.

And so, she goes, this life business finished;
Theirs is a griping regret.
The opportunity never to arise again.
And I feel their loss.

And my own.

Dianne Walters-Butler (copyright)

FLIGHT OF TERROR: HOSTAGE IN THE SKY

In June, 1985, my classmate, Father Jim McLoughlin, Pastor of St. Peter, Geneva, IL, and I led a pilgrimage to the Holy Land and Greece, the land of St. Paul's journeys. It was the dream of a lifetime for most in our group. A friend of ours, Father Tom Dempsey, St. Charles, was invited because he intended to lead a group from his own parish the following year. There were 33 of us altogether that boarded TWA flight #847 that Friday morning. This included Peter Hill, our tour director, who had led over 100 tours to Isreal from the U.S. with no previous incident of disruption. We had spent a wonderful week in Isreal. Then we flew to Athens. Having toured Athens and the ancient ruins of Corinth, we then embarked on a five day cruise of the Greek isles. This included Patmos where St. John, author of the 4th Gospel, had lived for a number of years. It also included the ruins of Ephesus in modern day Turkey to which St. Paul had written his epistle to the Ephesians.

Early Friday morning - on June the 14th - we disembarked in Pirraeus - port city for Athens. Our flight from Athens to Rome (TWA #847) was scheduled to depart at 8:55 a.m. It seemed to take the longest time for all our baggage to be delivered to our bus from the ship. Everyone was anxious not to miss the plane home. We arrived at the airport at 8:20 a.m. only to find out that the flight had been delayed to 9:35 a.m. What had happened was that another TWA flight to New York had had been cancelled that day. Therefore many of those passengers had been booked onto our flight, making it a full plane.

Later, I learned that the hijackers original plan had been to hijack the New York flight. Thus they were forced to change plans at the last minute, leaving one of the original 3 hijackers unable to board. We passed through two metal-detector security checks and finally boarded the plane. We took off at 9:55a.m. There were 153 people abooard the 727 aircraft (3 pilots, 5 flight attendants, 145 passengers including 2 hijackers and 33 of our group). We were 1/5th of the plane. Our director, Peter Hill, sat in the back row on the aisle seat. The two hijackers sat next to him. One (the taller man, Hassan Ezzedine) was already in place. The shorter one, Mohammed Ali Hamadi, then came on with a large carry-on bag. Just before take-off, the shorter man went to the toilet. Peter heard a sound, possibly shattering glass. In a Life magazine article, Peter offered the theory that the hijack weapons were concealed in a heavily-leaded glass container. The man returned to his place. Just a few minutes into our ascent, while the plane was still on an upward incline, the two men jumped over Peter Hill and ran up the aisle. I saw them run by and thought one was chasing the other. They banged on the cockpit door and shortly thereafter we heard the announcement of our being hijacked.

Then the terror began. People did not panic. There was no screaming and people were cooperative. First we were instructed to raise our hands over our heads. Later we were told to sit with our heads between our legs and our hands over our heads. A very painful position after a few hours! The shades were to be drawn and our passports handed in.

The flight attendants were instructed to surrender passports of military personnel, diplomats, and people with Jewish sounding names. Those who didn't cooperate fast enough or keep their heads low enough were smacked on the back of the head with the butt of the gun or the hijackers fist or open hand. The two hijackers paced up and down each holding a hand grenade and one also holding a pistol. We stared at the floor in silence. There was to be no talking.

The larger male passengers were moved into the middle and window seats; women moved to aisle seats. We soon realized that the two hijackers did not speak English. They knew only a few phrases. One spoke German. He was married to a German woman. Our flight burser, Uli Derrickson, spoke German so she became his interpreter.

Military personnel and those with Jewish sounding names were taken to the First Class Compartment and those in First Class were ushered back to the Coach. We did not know whom the hijackers represented. Were they acting on their own or were they part of some terrorist group? Only later did we learn they belonged to a radical fundamentalist group of Shiite Muslims, known as Hezbalah, who looked to the Ayatollah Khomeini of Iran as their idol. They were hopeful to have a similar type take-over of Lebanon and other Arab countries.

For the next 1 $1/2$ hours we passengers were terrorized. We had no idea where we were headed. The hijackers proceeded to pistol-whip Flight Officer Christian Zimmerman (who is an ordained Lutheran minister) to show they meant business. He happened to be closest to the cabin door. The crew were first told to fly to Algiers, a 4 hour flight. The hijackers were informed that there was only enough fuel for Rome or a city as close. They changed their order to Beirut.

We landed at the Beirut Airport at approximately 11:30 a.m. Seventeen older women and two children were released. They had no idea where they were going when they slid down the emergency chute. Sirens were going! It was awful for them!

The plane was refueled. Two hours later, more or less, we took off for Algiers, Algieria (five hours and two time zones away). We sat on the runway in Algerian heat for five hours. We were still sitting in that painful position (head-between-our-legs-hands-over-our-head). Permission had to be sought to go to the toilet. The toilet door had to be left open. People were embarrassed. Some later became ill.

The hijackers issued their demands to the airport personnel. They wanted the release of 700 Lebanese held in Isreal in return for our release. Kurt Carlson, a military reserve of Rockford, IL, was beaten severely. Then 21 more hostages were released. They included older women and children. We were now down to 111 hostages. At 8:30 p.m. Algiers time (10:30 p.m. Athens time) we took off again. I had a personal fear we would go to Libya and Mommar Khadafy. We actually headed back to BEIRUT. We all knew death could occur at any time. These were desperate men, running up and down, each with a hand grenade and one with a pistol. They were fanatically dedicated to their cause.

For me the closest brush with death occurred as we were about to land at the Beirut Airport the second time. During the flight I read from the New Testament. In the front pages I discovered a beautiful prayer called The Universal Prayer. It was attributed to Pope Clement XI. I had never seen the prayer before that I could recall but as I read it, I realized how apropos it was to the situation we were in. The Lord had graced me with its wisdom! Several of its paragraphs leapt off the page at me, so appropropriate were they. Here are those particular paragraphs...

I offer you, Lord, my thoughts: to be fixed on you;
my words: to have you for their theme;
my actions: to reflect my love for you;
my sufferings: to be endured for your greater glory.

I want to do what you ask of me:
in the way you ask,
for as long as you ask,
because you ask it...(this paragraph I had to read several
times to make it my own)

Teach me to realize that this world is passing,
that my true future is the happiness of heaven,
that life on earth is short,
and the life to come eternal.

Help me to prepare for death
with a proper fear of judgment,
but a greater trust in your goodness.
Lead me safely through death
to the endless joy of heaven.

I also prayed the rosary. I especially meditated on the sorrowful mysteries of Jesus' life; His agony in the garden, the scourging at the pillar, the crowning with thorns, His carrying the cross, His crucifixion. I could hear screams from the First Class Compartment. They had decided to kill a crew member, but then realized they needed them all. So they turned to the military personnel. Robert D. Stethem was beaten savagely. We couldn't be sure of what was going on.

Soon we approached the Beirut Airport. Our captain announced that because we were low on fuel we may be forced to make a crash landing. The airport lights were out and trucks were parked across the runway. Either we had to land on the congested runway or land in the Mediterranean Sea. Unbeknownst to us, the pilot, John Testrake, was screaming at the airport officials..."They're beating the passengers! They're beating the passengers! We're coming in!" I prayed the *Memorare*, a beautiful prayer to the Blessed Mother for her intercession. Then I prayed the prayer of Jesus in the Garden of Gethsemene "Father if you will take away this cup, not my will but yours be done". I then surrendered myself to the Lord in total abandonment. Immediately a tremendous sense of peace came over me! It seemed only seconds when the pilot announced calmly..."I think if we circle one more time they'll turn on the lights and remove the barricades". God had delivered us from certain death. Through the grace of God I was never quite afraid in the same way again during the rest of the ordeal.

We landed in Beirut a second time. Supposedly when the hijackers' demand for the Amal Shiites to come aboard was not accepted, they shot and killed Robert Stethem. His beaten body was thrown on the tarmac. Navy diver, Robert Suggs, was to be the next victim. Supposedly Uli Derrickson intervened screaming,"Enough!" "Enough!" (I heard a muffled pop sound go off but I only knew of the death after I got off.) Seven or eight Amal Militia (fellow Shiites) then came on. They were our new captors! The leader spoke English. He harangued us. The two hijackers dissapeared to sleep. Seven or nine more passengers were removed. They were mostly military, but also a Greek singer and his secretary.

Once again the plane took off. It was back to Algeria. This, however, we did not know. Now the searching and pillaging began. We were all called forward to the First Class Compartment. We were stripped of our billfolds, jewelry, flight bags. Everything was dumped in a big pile. The jewelry and valuables were put in a flight bag and promised to be returned. They never were. One captor took my rosary and put it around his neck. I protested vehemently to his superior. He was asked to remove it and he threw it on the pile.

It occurred to me that a week before our pilgrimage group had walked the Way of the Cross in Jerusalem. NOW we were living the Way of the Cross. (Jesus had been accused before Pilate...we too were condemned for things we never did; Jesus was stripped of his garments...we were stripped of our possessions; Jesus was mocked...We were severely criticized; Jesus was struck and tortured...some of us had the same happen to us; Jesus was condemned to death...we might also be.)

We landed at approximately 7:46 a.m. Algiers time. I was writing these times and incidents in a little notebook I had concealed. Later in the day 51 passengers including the flight attendants were exchanged for the third hijacker who had been left behind in the Athens Airport. The plane looked like a cyclone had hit it. Debris was scattered all about. Flightbags thrown about. Sometime around 10:00p.m. eight older men were released.

The 44 of us remaining were then ordered to the front of the coach section. The area was crowded and smoke-filled. Exhausted from little sleep and little food and feeling cramped, I walked past one of the guards and lay down across three empty seats in the back of the plane and fell asleep. No one disturbed me. When I awoke 3 or so hours later, there were 2 other passengers sitting across from me. They were feeling ill. The unoccupied seats were pushed foward making it evident from the rear which seats were occupied for an assassination if needed. I was informed that the plane had been wired for a suicidal explosion if demands were not met.

A Red Cross official came on board. He dialogued with the militia leaders. I signaled that the 2 men next to me were ill. The official then came to us and announced to us to follow him. I thought he had negotiated the release of all. Instead only the 3 of us were released. Grateful to God for my release, I promised myself I would do all I could to help comfort the already released passengers in Algiers and later Paris where we were all assembled plus work for the release of those still held captive.

I had the opportunity to make appeals on all the major TV networks. Two other passengers with medical problems were then released. Finally all our prayers were answered! All the remaining passengers - who had been taken back to Beirut for another 2 weeks - were released. What wonders had been wrought through the power of so many people praying across America and throughout the world. Till my dying breath, my heart will be filled with gratitude to God and to all my prayerful benefactors!

Father William McDonnell

Thanksgiving

I have always loved this time of year. I love the music, the food, the friendships, the memories and the stories, especially the stories. I have always loved the stories about miracles, from "It's a Wonderful Life," "A Christmas Carol" and "How the Grinch Stole Christmas" to the greatest miracle of all and our reason for the Christmas season.

However, during this past month, I have been personally involved in several miracles in my own life. And I'd like to share them with you for two reasons. First, because you are all a large part of these miracles and second, because I hope I can share some of the joy that I have felt during these last few weeks.

On Sunday, November 3, in the early hours of the morning, a fire started in my home. The fire started in the basement and crept up through the walls of our old home. We were all in bed, sound asleep. Our fire alarms did not go off, even though they had been tested last month. So, smoke started to fill our home and make its way up to the second floor.

The first miracle occurred when a little kitten, we had just adopted on Tuesday, cried loud enough to wake up my ten-year-old son, David. David sat up in bed to be met with smoke. He grabbed the kitten to his chest, had the soundness of mind to climb to the floor and crawl toward my husband and my bedroom. He was calling out, "Mom, Mom" as he crawled and that alerted our seventeen-year old daughter, Jennie, to the problem. Between the two of them, they woke up Nathan, Katie, Sarah, Andrew, Richard and me. We turned on the lights and rushed downstairs. Chris, our fifteen-year-old son, had fallen asleep on the couch, so we ran to wake him up. Then we hurried everyone out the door and into the car in front of the house.

Richard and I ran back in, grabbed some blankets, called 9-1-1 and left the house.

After we drove the car into our next door neighbor's driveway, we realized that our finches and Arlo, Chris's guinea pig, were still in the house, By this time we could see the flames in the basement and knew that we could not go back in. Richard went back to stand in front of the house and I stayed with the children, the kitten, one barn cat, and our old English Sheepdog in the station wagon.

Within a few minutes two officers from the Stephenson County Sheriff's Department arrived. They set up flares and helped direct the fire engines to the right place. But, beyond doing their "official" duties, one of these men gave Richard his coat in the sub-freezing weather, so he could stay warm. They also stayed with him, offering him moral support and answering his questions.

Minutes after their arrival the Cedarville and Lena Volunteer Fire Departments arrived, in fire trucks and their own personal vehicles. These fine people had jumped out of their beds to help save our home. They were wonderful. They worked for hours battling the fire. One fireman heard we needed a diaper for Andrew, so he went in and found a few diapers and brought them to the car.

The folks from Leamon's Ambulance Service arrived on the scene and gave us extra blankets and things to drink. Someone found Richard a cellular phone to use, so he called the bishop of our church to let him know what happened. Within 45 minutes, Mark Hamer, the bishop of our church who lives in Baileyville, and Russell Mulnix, our home teacher, arrived on the scene. They offered us support and love. And the Hamers opened their home to us.

I drove the children out to Baileyville, hoping that I wouldn't get stopped for driving in my pajamas with no shoes on. We arrived at the Hamers at about 3:30 a.m. JoAnn Hamer had beds made up for all of us and was simmering some hot chocolate on the stove. Within minutes, the children were tucked in and sound asleep.

Some would think that this was the end of the miracles. After all, we all got out safely and had the tremendous help of many fine men and women. But this is where most of the miracles began. At 6:30 a.m., Ruth Ann Mulnix was at the door with a bag filled with toothbrushes, toothpaste and other personal supplies. Toothbrushes might seem like a small thing, (of course, buying toothbrushes for a family of nine is never a small thing), but it was nice to have these little incidental needs taken care of. By 6:45, our insurance agent, Rich Sokup, was not only responding to our needs, he was on the phone with the claims adjuster to have him out to the house by mid-morning Sunday morning. Then they started to arrive, vans and cars filled with friends - but also filled with bags and boxes of clothing, socks, shoes, coats, mittens, and most of all, love.

I had been able to control my emotions through the entire fire. But this outpouring of love overwhelmed me and brought tears to my eyes. The Hamer's living room looked like a clothing store. It was very similar to the ending scene of "It's a Wonderful Life." I would love to list all the people who gave us things, but there were so many that I'm afraid I would forget someone. I think Jennie summed it up best when she said, "Mom, I didn't realize how much we were loved."

The miracles continued.

We met with the claims adjuster at 11 a.m. After bringing us clothing, Debbie and Randy Hohmann brought their video recorder out to our house and taped the damage for us. The damage was amazing. The entire wall behind the couch, where Chris had fallen asleep, was now a charred skeleton and the floor in the same room was half gone. I don't think I realized how blessed we had been until I walked through the smoky remains of our home.

Still the miracles continued.

Matt Ensign called us at the Hamer's to tell us that when he told his parents about our fire, they offered us the use of their home. They had recently decided to spend the winter in Texas with some of their children and so would be away from their home for six months - about the same amount of time we needed. When we talked to Ace to iron out the details, he said that before he left he fixed up quite a few things in the house because he had a strong feeling that someone was going to be living in the house while they were away.

The Relief Society (the women's organization in our church) brought in meals for us. When you're dealing with so many different issues, it's hard to concentrate on the simple things you need to sustain you. It was a great relief to not have to worry about making dinner.

Monday moring we were able to bring the children to school. We stopped by the classrooms of the younger children and explained the situation to their teachers. Each teacher was so understanding and concerned for our family's welfare, it again brought tears to my eyes. (I really am not usually such a cry-baby.)

Ruth Ann called from the Journal Standard letting me know that the newsroom was quite concerned about us and wanted to know what they could do to help. I talked with Todd McKenna a little later that morning and he wrote the story. (It's a little strange to be on the other side of the pad of paper.) We also walked through the house with a contractor on Monday morning. To our amazement and delight (another miracle) Arlo had survived! The contractor, Nathan Meier, kept shaking his head and saying, "It's amazing more wasn't damaged. It's amazing everyone is safe."

We choose to place the words "a miracle" in place of "amazing."

Once the community knew about the fire, we were once again showered with calls of concern and love. Teresa Fyock told me that her daughter's Sunday School class had prayed for the Reid family. We could feel the prayers and the love.

We have learned several great lessons from this fire. We have learned that there are wonderful, generous and caring people all around us, ready and willing to lift us when we fall and comfort us when we weep. Our children have the great security knowing that they have a huge extended family in this community. We have learned the importance of service. It's much more comfortable being able to help others, than having to accept help for yourself and your family, but from the experience we've learned how to serve others better in the future.

And so, on this Thanksgiving Day, the Reid Family sends their heartfelt love and thanks to all of you, for your prayers, your concern, your love, and your generousity. Perhaps it's best said in the immortal words of Dicken's Tiny Tim, "God Bless You, every one!"

Terri Reid

6

Creativity in the Community

In order to create there must be a dynamic force, and what force is more potent than love?

Igor Stravinsky

The Little Road

How I love the little road
  That winds its peaceful way
Beyond our clover-scented fields
  A ribbon dusty-grey.

And sometimes when misfortune comes
  And twilight hovers low
I take my daughter's hand in mine
  And down the road we go.

The crickets sing a happy song
  A rabbit scurries by,
We find some berries on a bush,
  My little girl and I,

And all the world stands still, it seems
  To watch the firefly
Go flickering along that road
  Where sweet contentment lies.

It's good to have a little hand
  While I am in this world
It's good to have a little road
  To wander with my girl

And when she grows into her life
  If troubles come her way
I hope she has a little road
  To take at close of day.

I hope she has a little road
  To take at close of day.

Stella M. Jensen

Heartland Voices

Thank you to Olga Gize Carlile for writing about Daniel Smith and his work. Her column aroused enough of my curiosity that I decided to take a vacation day from work and attend the first "Voices of the Heartland," a Highland Community College poetry reading series.

My vacation day was definitely not wasted.

I cannot remember a time ever being so moved by anyone's use of the English language. Mr. Smith, using few, but descriptive words, brought a flood of recollections to my mind. I recalled childhood days long gone. I remembered relationships with people far removed from sight and sound who played small but vital roles in my life.

Listening to Mr. Smith, I learned I need to pay more attention to the subtle and less to the obvious. After all, when everything is said and done, very little in life and nature is truly obvious.

I found it impossible to hide my appreciation. After the reading I shook Mr. Smith's hand. The best adjective I could think of to describe what I had just heard was "incredible." A man sitting near the front approached and said he could tell I was listening intently; I suppose the smile on my face or perhaps the tear in my eye was evidence enough for him to draw a conclusion.

When my friend and companion for the evening asked what I thought of my first poetry reading, I could only answer her by muttering, "I had no idea...I had no idea." For me to be at a complete loss for words is itself a rare event. I always thought real excitement and intrigue could only be created by things moving at break-neck speeds or from rock concerts loud enough to cause permanent ear damage.

I guess while I was busy building up a huge tolerance for technicolor, I didn't notice my ability to imagine was quickly slipping away. I hope I don't ever take this priceless gift for granted again.

If someone would have told me just a short time ago that I would attend a poetry reading and then write about the awe it generated in me, I would have said he was crazy.

I am much too busy chasing down success and running up bills to take time out and listen to some silly words, I have my own life and my own concerns, thank you very much.

An accidental guest column in *The Journal-Standard* changed all of that though.

Today I own a dictionary, even if I did buy it second-hand. My love for words and their various purposes is growing daily thanks to many people and institutions.

While Mr. Smith and I don't have a lot of things in common, his poetry touched me at the very center of my soul. For maybe the first time in my life I was able to hear something I had never heard before – my own heart. Believe me, it sounded better than I ever dreamed it would. So thank you, Dan, and Highland Community College.

I am looking forward to the next "Voices of the Heartland."

I do have more vacation days left.

John Cook

Poetry is the opening and closing of a door, leaving those who look through to guess about what is seen during a moment.

Carl Sandburg

Field

I would like to have been
the man
who plowed this field,
so far back
in a seldom seen hollow
of southwestern Wisconsin's
unglaciated uplands.

I would like to have had
my hand
on the wheel,
turning the old Farmall
across the headlands
where the white birches
stand guard
before the dark pine woods.
And to have looked back,
over my shoulder,
as the moldboards
sliced into last year's crop,
turning the old under
to feed the new.

FOR THE LOVE OF COMMUNITY

I would like to have known
what he knew,
as the breath of new furrows
followed him, round
after round,
while the world spun on
in separate orbit
far beyond the hills,
leaving him
alone with his land,
doing just what needed
to be done.

I would like to have been
the man who plowed this field.

Dan Smith

Duane Smith

Words of Wit and Wisdom

As Mother's Day comes around this year it seemed natural to think of my own mother and her words of wit and wisdom. She seemed to have an endless number of sayings and homilies, which often come into my mind.

There were five girls in our family and she used to tell us, "You aren't beautiful and you aren't rich, so you'll have to be nice," meaning perhaps that that would get us through life. Also being nice meant being clean. She would remind us to wash our "grousty" elbows and put Honey and Almond cream on them. I've never found the word "grousty" in any dictionary.

We would always have a big outdoor picnic and play day on the Fourth of July. If it happened to rain (which it seldom did in Oklahoma) Mama would calm us down with this: "If it rains before seven, it stops before eleven." Then one of us would be sent out to watch the sky to try to see a patch of blue. If the patch of blue was big enough to "make a pair of Dutchman's britches," things would really clear up and the picnic was on!

Mama was always very supportive of our projects and if we happened not to succeed the first time, this was her advice: "Just keep on keeping on" because "there are ways to kill a cat rather than choking it on butter."

And my favorite phrase of encouragement which I find myself still using to tackle a difficult job is "like the hen ate the grindstone--a little at a time." Who knows what a grindstone is today?

When Mama was frustrated or disgusted she'd say, "Shoot a monkey." Where in the world this phrase came from we'll never know now. My older sisters used to give her kitchen gadgets, and my mother would say, "My, my, that's as handy as a pocket on a shirt."

When I began to take "domestic science" and to sew for my younger sisters and make some big mistake or sew a wrong seam Mama would say soothingly, "It'll never be noticed on a galloping horse." Or, "Oh, well, you can't get all the possums up one tree."

If we were trying to hurry her, Mama would answer, "All right, I'll be there in two shakes of a dead sheep's tail."

Mama's advice was to get along with people. "Tis better to have the good will of a dog, than the ill will." In assessing people's clothing, she would say, "Remember, many a noble heart beats beneath a rusty jacket."

Mama always arose early, and when she felt it was time for the family to be up and about she'd start singing. In our room she'd sing an old tune whose words went like this: "Wake up, Jacob, day's a-breaking, squirrels in the trees with their tails a-shaking."

As she grew older and the grandchildren started coming, each last one was the cutest, smartest, and prettiest child on God's earth! I can see her holding one in her arms, patting the baby's chubby bare feet and saying, "Shoe the horse, shoe the mare, but let the coltie's feet go bare."

One of my younger sisters took our older son, then about four, to visit with his grandmother. Our favorite good laugh today is when my mother said to my sister, "Betty, see what that child is crying for and give it to him," all in the same breath.

Today as I contemplate these sayings of hers I realize how wise and sound my mother's philosophy was. Such small words and such basic rules for living.

Wherever my mother is, I'm sure she is making it a brighter and more joyful place as she always did for her family and friends.

Virginia Babcock

Kenneth Fissell

I belive in the incomprehensibility of God.

Honore de Balzac

Beyond Our Comprehension

To Lori from Aunt Gertie

If the earth were as small as the moon, the power of gravity would be too weak for the needs of man. If the earth were as large as Jupiter, Saturn, or Uranus, the power of gravity would be too strong.

If the oceans were one half their present size, we would have only one half the rainfall we now enjoy. If the oceans were an eighth larger, our rainfall would increase four times making the earth a swamp that would make man's habitation on earth impossible.

If the earth were as far from the sun as Mars, there would be freezing snow and ice every twenty-four hours or every night.

The solar power of the sun controls freezing to sustain life on earth, making solar energy that is greater than one thousand Niagaras available to man.

If the earth would rotate on its axis one hundred miles per hour, instead of the approximate one thousand miles per hour, it would burn and freeze alternately each day resulting in no vegetation on earth.

When making the earth and everything in it, God put salt in the oceans to regulate freezing therefore adjusting the ice accumulation in the polar regions over the centuries.

A wealth of knowledge of God's creative power removes all doubt that He gave life to the mighty oceans, power and nature on earth. That confirms all facts of a mighty, influential, sympathetic, and benevolent power so great it is beyond our comprehension.

The ships and the whale alike play in the mighty oceans; all of these depend on God to supply their daily needs and food. He opens His hand wide to feed them from his daily, bountiful provision. (Psalms 104:24-28)

Full of honor and majesty are His work, His righteousness endures forever. (Psalms 111:3)

Gertrude Stees

The Bridge Building

An old man, going a lone highway
came at the evening, cold and gray,
to a chasm, vast and deep and wide
through which was flowing a sullen tide.
The old man crossed in the twilight dim;
that sullen stream had no fears for him.
But he turned, when he reached the other side,
and built a bridge to span the tide.
"Old man," said a fellow pilgrim near,
"You are wasting strength in building here.
Your journey will end with the ending day:
You never again must pass this way
You have crossed the chasm, deep and wide,
Why build you the bridge at the eventide?"
The old man lifted his old gray head.
"Good friend, in the path I have come," he said.
"There followeth after me today
A youth whose feet must pass this way.
This chasm that has been naught to me
to that fair haired youth may a pitfall be.
He, too, must cross in the twilight dim.
Good friend, I am building the bridge for him."

Will Allen Dromgoole

The Valley of Yesterday

Out of the valley of yesterday
With its sorrow and vain regret,
I go as a traveler who makes her way
In haste, ere the sun shall set

Bright is the city of dreams--come--true
Over the mountain's brim,
Fame and fortune and friendships new--
But turning, my eyes grow dim.

And I gaze on the valley of yesterday,
Back to a springtime young
When I used to laugh at the things you'd say
And life was a song unsung.

Fair is the city of dreams--come--true,
Glimmer and glint and power,
But I'd barter it all just to walk with you
In yesterday's golden hour.
How we dipped them in ink
As they dangled in front of us there.

Spring air spins a spell
That feels simply swell
Each Saturday night on the street
When the stores on each side
Fling their doors open wide
And the farmers do their trading and meet.

There's a street, warm and kind
Where someday I'll find
The dreams of my girlhood still wait,
Unchanging and true,
Like the friends that I knew
In the days when just living felt great.

Stella M. Jensen

The wisest men follow their own direction.

Euripides

Resolutions to Keep

Each in our own fashion
Spread Goodwill at Christmas "Time"
We give to church or charities
Some money or in "Kind"

We should continue giving
Throughout all the "Year"
Because this famine quickly strikes
Feast over cupboard "bare"

To our favourite charities
Extend a helping "hand"
Volunteer your time each week
And offer to pay the "Band"

Let's keep the Christmas Spirits
In our hearts all through each "Month"
When Christmas once again arrives
We'll be a Happy "Bunch"

Sidney Frederick

To a person in love, the value of the individual is intuitively known. Love needs no logic for its mission.

Charles A. Lindbergh

Rocky, Bullwinkle and Thou

I remember the exact moment I first fell in love. It was that laugh. I hated it. I shouldn't have been surprised when I picked up the phone to discover the voice of a friend telling me a piece of important news. With the proper tact and consideration one should expect of an old friend, he told me the woman who lead me through my first, and maybe greatest romance, has finally consented to a proposal of marriage.

I began thinking about what love has added to my life as well as my own small contributions to its continued existence. I've thought about how the love of family members and close friends can support us in our most troubled times. I've thought about how romantic love adds such brilliant color and subtle textures to the fabric of life.

And I thought about that laugh, again. I can't say I ever loved Jackie's laugh but it was a laugh that made me love her.

We were young, Duran Duran and Michael Jackson were inescapable voices on the radio, and the scourge of humanity, the minivan, had yet to roll off an assembly line. I was absolutely dashing with my thick, long hair tucked into my Indiana Jones fedora (at some point I lost the hair and the hat) as I drove my Pinto station wagon (it died) along the shore of Lake Tahoe. Man, I was bad. I can understand why she loved me. If I could have break danced, I would have been perfect.

Jackie had a beautiful, round, Irish face, deep, black hair and startling bright blue eyes. Her calm, soft voice was always a soothing tonic. And, she had a "come hither" look that turned my legs into room-temperature Jell-O and disconnected my spinal cord from my brain. But after six months of dating I knew something wasn't right.

It was that noise.

It was one of those strange and unsettling assortment of sounds Jackie made whenever she laughed. Since she was a good natured person Jackie laughed frequently. Whenever Jackie began to cut loose, I wanted to take cover, leave the room or pretend that I didn't know who she was. At the onset of one of her full-blown paroxysms Jackie would begin exhaling large quantities of air while making absolutely no sound whatsoever. Then, about the time a mortal would pass out, she would take a deep breath to try to regain her composure. She never did succeed. The resulting noise was a cross between a 1957 Chevy needing a tune up, and a rusty, out-of-control chain saw cutting a wet log.

Up to, and including the evening where fate awaited us in a darkened theater, I tried very hard not to be funny, kept her away from comedy films, and I feigned disinterest in watching Saturday morning cartoons with her. When she did laugh, I waited anxiously for her to inhale. When that moment arrived, I coughed, whistled, made noises with my armpit, anything I could do to try to cover that racket of hers.

But I always felt a twinge of guilt afterward. I felt it was wrong to want to strangle her every single time she found something that amused her.

However, everything was about to change.

It was a surprisingly cold, dry, late-spring Friday night. We made plans to go to Reno and watch a Rocky and Bullwinkle cartoon festival (long before its appearance on videotape), which made the evening the social event of the year; of course, it was still early in the year.

I'm not sure what caused my change of heart that night. Maybe it was the combination of popcorn, the funniest moose on film and the sugar rush from sticking 14 pounds of JuJu Bees to my fillings. Whatever happened to me that night, I had no control over it.

Once in Reno, we went directly to our destination, the Keystone Theater. The large, darkened theater was full of like-minded people with the same bad taste we possessed. The two of us managed to comfortably seat ourselves in the exact center of the movie theater, where I (normally) liked to sit.

Shortly after the animated action began on screen, Jackie began to chuckle at the antics of Boris and Natasha. I slumped in my seat and sat dreading the onset of that dreadful noise. Given our seating situation, I knew I was trapped like a caged animal with nowhere to hide. I swallowed hard. She inhaled normally. I exhaled normally. I relaxed and refocused my attention on the cartoon.

I wish that I could remember at this late date exactly what triggered this particular bout of Jackie's laughter, but my memory fails me. What I do remember, however, is an overwhelming feeling of terror at the first rumblings of the coming sonic earthquake.

But when it hit I didn't get the heebee-geebees. Instead, I lost all of my considerable cool and fell into my own convulsions of laughter. In an instant I had jets of ice-cold Pepsi streaming out of my nose. Jackie lost all control when she witnessed my dating faux pas. I had hot tears streaming down my face. I couldn't draw a breath, and Jackie was making a terrible racket. Not only did the engine of her 1957 Chevy sound especially out of tune, it sounded as though her muffler was shot, too. The harder I laughed, the harder Jackie laughed, and that caused her to make even more terrible sounds.

We attracted the attention of more than a few theater patrons. They, however, were not as amused as the two of us. We were feeling the stares of a hundred strangers, but it hardly mattered anymore; we were on a roll. I tried to be cool but a second burst of Pepsi shot up and out my nose. My side ached, but I felt wonderful. I stared at Jackie's raspberry-red, tearstained cheeks, her contorted face and I was stunned. Suddenly she was the most beautiful woman my eyes had ever touched.

After the movie ended, peeved patrons shuffled past us and muttered curses at us. But, I looked into the mascara-streaked face of the woman smiling at me, both of us too embarrassed to speak, and I knew I loved her.

Thank you Jackie.

Gregory Douglas

Waste: To Spend or Use Carelessly

And shall we waste it, then,
    this present, day?
A gift that's wrapped in clouds
    and tied with strings of sun,
And handed to us, free?

Let's listen to its winds
    insist, "Throw wide your arms
    and savor it."

Let's let its presence
    wind bright scarves of thought
    about our minds.

And then let's share
    this present, day...
A "loaves and fishes" sharing
    which makes the gift expand
To fill the heart with hope.

Leone Castell Anderson

The more that you read,
The more that you will know.
The more that you learn,
The more places you'll go.

Theodore Geisel (Dr. Seuss)

Words

Poetry to me, as expressed in the oh, so beautifully written words of the great poets, has always seemed like music. If you give yourself and your feelings over to it, poetry, like music, can exhilarate, soothe, sadden or make you want to laugh or cry. Loving it, even as a child, and reading everything I could get my hands on, it is not surprising I wanted to write it. And write it I did, for all of my life.

When I was young, I was always so pleased that the teachers included what I had written in the monthly school newspaper, when I could help write the plays we used to give almost every Friday afternoon as a special treat. When older, I was even more pleased when friends told me they liked what I had written.

I am always especially pleased when people who do not usually read poetry tell me they understand what I am saying and enjoy it. No hidden meanings to search out, no special training necessary, just enjoyment and understanding. Could an amateur ask for more?

Instead of bedtime stories I often recited poetry to my children, my own and poems I had loved and memorized as a child. I have always had a strong belief that if you can interest children in literature you never have a child who is a complete failure in school. One of the first children's poems I wrote was a favorite of my children, and is also one of my grandchildren's:

Whenever I learn to Read

I can go to Timbuctoo,
  To Mandalay and China, Too,
The Spanish Main and Borneo,
    There's just no place that I can't go
    Whenever I learn to read!

I can see the hills of France
   And Ireland where the fairies dance,
The blue skies o're the blue Pacific,
   I'll see things strange and terrific
   Whenever I learn to read!

I can walk with Daniel Boone,
   Ride beneath a Hunter's Moon,
Sail with pirates, find a treasure,
   Anything can be my pleasure
   Whenever I learn to read!

Then it comes, first day of school!
   But it seems so very cruel,
Teacher says, "Not ready yet!"
   I must learn the Alphabet
Before I learn to read!

But I'll be patient and I'll be good
   And I'll do all the things I should,
And then before me, all unfurled,
   Will be the whole wide wonderful world
   Whenever I learn to read!

I was a child during the Depression years and my proud German father did not believe in charity, so we "got along" on our own, on what we had. Later, when his health failed, I was the only one working in the family and the struggle to educate myself took up any spare time I had. I was then and still am a voracious reader, but it is easier to snatch time for reading out of a too - full schedule than it is to find the quiet time necessary to develop thoughts into words with meaning. Still later, marriage, five children, working as an accountant with my husband in our own firm. . .the ambition I had felt so strongly was put on "hold."

About ten years ago my husband had a heart attack, with many complications and with steadily deteriorating health. We sold our business, I got another job and finally retired when it was necessary for him to go on kidney dialysis, which I did in our home.

Many times during those ten years he went to the border of that "undiscovered country from which no traveler returns." He had somehow pulled back, until finally there was no return for him.

I remember his wake, not as a sad time, but as a time when I felt pride while listening to all the good things people had to say about him, how much they liked him. I found myself wishing he could have been there, really been there, himself. A strange thought indeed! But he had always enjoyed talking to people - anyone, anytime, anywhere. The word friendly described him better than any other word I can think of.

The day of his funeral is a complete blank to me. I don't recall it at all, except for shaking uncontrollably at the graveside services. Reality had set in and my mind was numb. Frederic Lawrence Knowles wrote, "Joy is a partnership. Grief weeps alone." I think this is true for even those who seek out grief therapy must finally come to their acceptance alone.

For a long time afterward I did what my father had always said could get you through anything - just put one foot in front of the other and keep walking. I took care of all the financial problems, sorted through what seemed like endless medical bills with so many errors due to complicated and many treatments. I listened to so much advice, conflicting often, and suddenly I sat down and took a good hard look at reality.

Reality was. . . . .I was alone. All the people who had been so supportive, so caring, so <u>there</u> had to go back to their own life.

I looked at my life.

Reality was, my life had "gone by." I felt like crying. I did cry! Where had all those years gone? What had happened to all those lovely dreams I had dreamed while lying under the lilac bushes on hot, lazy summer afternoons, when the future was limitless as those blue skies so far above me?

The answer was - Life. Life had happened! As it does, as it must, as it always will. I thought of the irony of it. I, who so loved the written word, who felt I had something and wanted something worth saying, had spent my life as an accountant.

A good, solid, respectable worthwhile vocation, to be sure, but completely opposite to what I had wanted to do.

There was drama, if you like that kind!

I immediately felt sorry for myself of course. That was when I wrote my poem "Dreams." It fit perfectly the mood I had allowed myself to sink into. Here it is. You will see what I mean.

Dreams

When I was young and my life was new
There were so many things that I had to do;
So many places for me to go,
So many things that I had to know.

So much laughter and so many tears
Waiting for me in the coming years.
So many dreams to make come true,
For I was young and my life was new.

But, too many places for me to go,
Too many things for my heart to know the laughter came and
       I had tears
As I walked through life in those long, long years.
I searched but couldn't quite make come true
All those dreams I had when my life was new;
But I kept on searching around each bend.
Never admitting the road would end.

Now, no more places for me to go,
No more things for my heart to know.
The laughter's an echo, the tears have dried;
All the lovely dreams have been set aside.
My eyes grow dim and my memory, too.
The roads to travel are very few.
I can only turn to the setting sun,
For I am old my life is done.

I have never felt sorry for myself very long, and I didn't this time either. In a life filled with perhaps a little more than my share of "bad times" I always made myself look around at others, and I could generally find others far worse off than me. This really does work!

That, and asking God not to take away all my troubles with a flick of celestial magic, but to give me strength to work through this. He had never failed to answer that prayer for me.

I looked back at the past, the good times. And, oh, they were there! Not round the world trips, or grand balls or little thousand dollar things, but the sharing and the caring were real and dear and meant so much more.

I wrote two more of my poems then, and they come from the heart. Not Keats or Lord Byron, but somehow they define what I am.

THREE LOVES

Three loves had I in my lifetime,
Each one held so dear and so true.
Each had his own special place in my heart,
And each of you know I loved you.

My first love. . .oh, how special it was,
like a rocket went off in my heart!
I walked on air, I waltzed on a cloud;
We could barely stand being apart.
A kiss, a touch, a lingering look
Sent chills racing up, down my spine.
Each moment away from him seemed like forever.
I dreamed only of when he'd be mine.

My second love? Tranquil, contented, so sure,
So steady, so dear, and such pride!
That you were my own, we were truly as one,
Facing all of life's trials side by side.
No trouble could touch me for long with you near.
We each seemed one half of the whole.
We were friends, we were lovers; truly
As if we two shared but one soul.

My last love? Perhaps best of all,
All the sweeter for being the last.
It held all the best, the sum of my life:
It was present, and future, and past.
This love would endure till the sun grew cold
And the stars disappeared from the sky;
Till all of the things I had known were no more,
Till the day of our judgment was nigh.

Three loves had I in my lifetime. . .
They had to be part of God's plan,
For the name and the face of all three were the same.
They belong to only one man.

WALTZ AGAIN WITH ME

We waltzed when first we met. Do you remember?
The music never stopped our whole life through.
Whether happy, sad or sweetly sentimental I loved it, for I listened,
    dear, with you.

Now you are gone. I shall hear no more, this music.
Is this all? Silence, for all eternity?
I cannot believe tis. Somewhere.....out there...
We shall meet and you will waltz again with me

Betty Mandt

7

Community History and Community Spirit

The only ones among us who will be really happy are those who will have sought and found how to serve.

Albert Schweitzer

It should be the historian's business not to belittle but to illuminate the greatness of man's spirit.

C.V.Wedgwood

A Visit From Buffalo Bill

This is a short story that happened when our family lived in Freeport's east side neighborhood, about 1915.

One day, a fine looking gentleman came to the door; he was from the circus. His rap was answered by my mother. He asked her if she had a bath tub, he would like to take a bath, a good old fashioned bath. My mother said she didn't have a store bought tub but showed him what she had. It was a big wooden tub made of red cedar and when you got through you smelt like pine needles. He thought that would be great.

She told him to come back in an hour and she would have things all ready for him. She had us pump soft water from the cistern and then she heated it in the spring or summer kitchen. She had a big bar of homemade soap and when he came back he took his bath in the summer kitchen. He sang all the while he was bathing. He took his time and when he got through he was a polished gentleman. My mom told him how nice he looked. He had a coat of doe skin with Indian artwork all over it. It was really beautiful. Us kids all said how nice he looked, then he reached into his pocket and gave my mom a silver dollar and introduced himself as Buffalo Bill. We were so stunned we all looked at each other and said, "'Buffalo Bill, oh my!" Then he gave us all a ticket to the Wild West Show. Now, that was a thrill of a lifetime.

I am nearly 90 now and I still can see the expression on my sister's face. We all went to the show and my mom framed the silver dollar. Now, this is a true story, believe it or not.

I was so proud to have had Buffalo Bill use our old bath tub, I had to tell everyone. They wouldn't believe me, but I told them to ask my mom and she would show them her silver dollar hanging on the wall. I think she had Buffalo Bill's signature on the back of the frame. She cut it out of a wild west magazine.

Now, you ask, what did you do before TV and radio—we always had things popping up somewhere.

Margaret Bruince McCaffrey
as told to: Roger Hill

Getting Involved

Participation is the name of the Game.
Whatever the primary objective
Stand up and be counted; it's your world, too.
Be never subdued, nor defeated.

My personal view is keep fit and enthused;
Take active part in the project;
An active part in word and deed—
And never lose sight of the object.

Twenty four hours is the span of our being,
When working and sleeping or playing and eating.
Whatever you do, the task must prove pleasant;
That is involvement, our living at present.

There will be no time for idle regrets—
We might have done this, or we should have done that.
The mere fact of our implementation
We are doing the best, for this our great nation.

I will close now, and adhere to a creed:
Being involved, in most of the "Deeds."

Sidney Frederick

The direction in which education starts a man or woman, will determine his or her future.

Plato

Beginnings

This is a brief history of some of the factors that led to the formation of Freeport Community College and later, Highland Community College.

My involvement begins in the late 1940's when the Freeport Board of Education asked me to start an adult education program. After setting up a broad-based advisory committee and surveying the community, we set up a series of classes to meet once a week for eight weeks in the fall of 1949.

The response was greater than anticipated. We sponsored another set of classes in the spring of 1950. Within a year we had an enrollment of over 1,000 students.

The advisory committee now wondered about the possibility of forming a community college in Freeport. To assist in getting facts, I attended a summer course on community colleges at the University of California in Berkeley. The instructor, Dr. Leland Medsker, asked Freeport to participate in a study of a community which had no community college. We did. Other communities in the study had community colleges or other forms of higher education.

One of the results of the study showed that communities with a community college had sixty to eighty percent of their students continuing their education. In Freeport, less than a third of students continued their education. Dr. Medsker came to Freeport twice to explain to interested citizens the importance of a community college in a community.

Many Freeport citizens now became interested in the idea of a community college. Among the people promoting the community college were Don Opel, Judge Marvin Burt and Louis Neyhart. The Freeport Board of Education asked the University of Illinois to evaluate if it was feasible for the district to establish a community college.

The study indicated it was possible for the district to establish a community college. In 1961, the voters approved a tax levy and a building expansion at the high school. In 1962, the Freeport Community College would be established with an enrollment of 300 students. Classes were held in the high school from 4 to 10 p.m. The movement from a local community college soon began. We now have Highland Community College with a campus including many fine buildings which serves the entire area.

Reuben Baumgartner

Duane Smith

Acres for Education
Acquisition of the 210 Acre HCC Campus

In 1962, at the urging of Mr. Donald Breed, publisher of the Freeport Journal Standard, I ran for the Freeport District 145 Board of Education and won.

At that time, the Freeport Community College was just forming under Dean Earl Hargett. Our board was also the junior college board and Supt. David Ponitz, was our leader. Classes were held after hours in the high school which the college soon outgrew. It then moved into a vacant insurance building at the corner of Locust and Stephenson Streets.

We all knew this was only temporary and were looking for a permanent campus. Nothing ideal was apparent. Then one Saturday evening at a cocktail party at Don Breed's home, Bill Koenig approached me with the news that "the Best farm" was being sold to a developer and that the closing was early next week. This was a choice site for the college.

I excused myself, went into the house and called attorney John Korf, also a member of the school-college board. I asked John to contact Grace Best Taft, widow of Dr. C.I. Best and explain to her that she could keep $25,000 more in her pocket by selling her farm to the college foundation than to the developer because of capital gains tax savings. The law allowed for that at the time.

John said, "we don't have enough money to buy the farm," to which I responded, "No , but we have enough to purchase an option. Go make the deal."

This was in August of 1965. We formed our committee, which I chaired, and set our plans to "sell" the campus to the public by private subscription. David Ponitz coined the name for our appeal "Acres for Education." We paid $435 per acre for the 210 acres for a total of $91,350. Grace Best Taft donated the most valuable 40 acres to our foundation at a ripe appraised price, then sold the balance at $91,350, which produced a tax deduction and saved her about $25,000. (The tax law has since been changed.)

We price tagged each acre at $500 to cover our costs and hopefully enhance foundation assets. Each donation was awarded a printed pressed-board plaque with a little plastic box of "Acres for Education" dirt on it.

The response was overwhelming. Individuals, organizations and even card clubs took up their own collections to "buy" an acre. Our largest donor bought 5 acres for $2,500.

By late October, we were over goal after only 4 weeks of our appeal. The committee decided to continue until Thanksgiving to acquire development funds, and then make this a presentation to the Freeport community as a Christmas present.

Unfortunately, news was leaked and the headline "College Campus Over Goal," lead to our contributions diminishing. We were $40,000 over goal at that time which converted to 92 acres over goal.

No one offered a word of criticism. I'm sure that each donor, when he or she sets foot on the HCC campus thinks, "I'm walking on my acre."

I know I do.

Thomas Ennenga

How the Stephenson County Fair Began

A.J. Hill, Raymond Kerch, and I were very active in a Rabbit Club in the 1920's. We were raising high quality rabbits for their fur and for the meat, which was popular at the time. Silver fox furs were all the rage then, and we were trying to find a breed of rabbit that could match the silver fox's pelt. We also had Silver Fox Ranch with one hundred and fifty pairs of silver foxes. I'm digressing, however.

We developed a plan to stage a large rabbit show and went to the Park Board to find out if we could use Taylor Park for the show. We found them to be enthusiastic about the idea. Mr. Roy Bowers, an executive of the electric company, was on the Park Board, and was an ardent supporter of the show. We decided to have booths at the show and sell space to companies that wished to display their supplies that were used in the rabbit business. The booths sold well and helped to defray some of the costs.

People were hungry for entertainment. They especially wanted a place to take their children. They loved the rabbits. Many people were unaware of the wide variety of rabbits and the specialty breeds that were being displayed. The exhibitors were pleased with the number of people visiting their booths. Their was no charge for admission for the show. People could come in and browse at their leisure. Overall, the first show was a huge success. More people showed up than could be accommodated. My father and Mr. Bowers were very happy, even though they didn't make a dime. There was a nice write up in the newspaper. Many of the rabbits were sold. A larger show was planned for the following year.

We invited the 4-H Club to exhibit at the show. A large tent was rented to cover the exhibition booths, which were leased to companies like Rawleigh's, Furst McNess, and Hillmer's Rabbit Suppliers. Many women exhibited their wares and crafts. My father was the first to suggest that we could possibly start a fair. "Let's call it Stephenson County Fair," he suggested. That would eventually become the name of our annual fair in the county.

World War II started and we were unable to have the fair for the next three years. Dad and Roy Bowers spoke with the Farm Bureau and asked them to consider taking over the responsibilities for the fair. They were reluctant at first, but said that they would consider it. Mr. Scheider of the Farm Bureau was in favor of the idea and persuaded them to try it. They surveyed the area and found an ideal location. Their ideal spot is where the Stephenson County Fairgrounds stand today.

The new fair directors decided that they would have to charge admission in order to develop the grounds and establish permanent buildings for the fair. A midway was established during the first year at the new location. Larger crowds began showing up at the fair. Their enthusiasm and encouragement has continued to grow over the years and the fair has expanded to meet the people's needs. Attendance records are now set annually. The Fair Board continues looking for ways to make the fair bigger and better each year. The entertainment that performs each year are national and international stars. Everyone looks forward to the Stephenson County Fair each year during the third week of August.

As the Ferris Wheel's lights shine during the night and the sounds of happy children on the rides emanate from the corner of Walnut and Fairgrounds Roads, I think back to the simple start to the fair. The volunteers that work hard each year are to be commended for their efforts, today. I especially remember those that were there in the beginning. The original group that developed the fair are all gone now, except for me. They would be proud of the Stephenson County Fair!

Roger Hill

Kenneth Fissell

Jane Addams Land Park Foundation and the Growth of Oakdale Park

In 1970, Judge Marvin Burt, a veteran Freeport Park Commissioner, in company with Mr. James Locke, Michael Cassidy, and other park proponents, incorporated a non-profit, tax-exempt foundation. The foundation's purpose was to acquire future park lands as they became available. Sadly, such lands had already been purchased by the time the need arose.

The foundation was inspired by the success of Mr. John Rutherford of Peoria, a close friend of Marvin Burt. I was in New York City when a call came from Jim Locke asking me to join them as a founding trustee. I was honored to accept their invitation.

The foundation slowly began gathering properties. The first was Thomas Wohlford Park at Buena Vista by gift of his decendants. This was followd by the gift of five acres of virgin, dry prairie adjacent to the Freeport Raceway Park.

Stephenson County gave us the Indian Gardens Tract when they sold the Count Farm. They also sold us an access right-of-way. A ten acre timber at the eastern edge of our county was bequeathed to the foundation later. Most notable was the growth of Oakdale Park from twenty-seven acres to its present size of 133 acres. This is the largest of the Freeport Parks.

In the early part of the twentieth century, the Evangelical Reformed Church operated Oakdale as a summer Bible study camp complete with dormitories and swimming pool. This twenty-seven acre, beautiful wooded park fell into disuse. It was then acquired by the Freeport Park District. It continued as a nature study area with educational material and displays in the former dormitory-dining building, but it needed to be bigger and better.

The fifty acres adjacent to the south border were owned by Edward Page Meyers, a local gentleman living in Denver, who kept it as a hobby farm. Gordon Hunter was appointed as his Illinois attorney upon Mr. Meyers' death in 1981. I was president of the foundation at the time. Mr. Hunter called to inform me that the fifty acres should be joined to Oakdale. I told him that I would see what I could do.

The Park Board was very enthusiastic about this possibility. They said that they could apply for a state matching grant, but that they would still want to purchase it when they could accumulate the funds.

We contacted the First National Bank. They promised a loan for seventy-five percent of the purchase price, if I could supply acceptable personal guarantees for the balance. I was able to produce these guarantees within thirty minutes. The loan was made on the property and the foundation took title. The loan provided a balloon payment of all interest on the last payment. The Park Board did get the state funds, paid the bank, and owned the property. The foundation was able to purchase the land without actually paying any money out-of pocket. The park had blossomed into seventy-seven acres.

Mary Brown Lamm owned the twenty-two acre tract of land just west of the park. There would be no access to the recently acquired land west of Crane's Creek without her consent. Mrs. Lamm had spoken of selling her land for years, but had not taken any definitive action. Mr. Woody Burt called me one day out of the blue to inform me that she might be interested in selling. He said, "We don't have enough money to buy it." "Yes," I said, "but we have enough for an option." We had approximately $9,000 in the treasury. Woody offered a deal that we get a qualified appraisal of the land and offer her that amount. The appraisal was for $75,000. This included a small house, a ramshackle corn crib, nine acres of plow ground and the remainder was scrubby second growth timber. She accepted our offer, so we got busy in our appeal for the money.

Our earliest efforts garnered a $25,000 leadership gift. One of the trustees added $40,000 and several other trustees offered a total of an additional $12,000. We were almost there, when I received a telephone call at my place of business. "Hello, Tom, this is Harry Buss." I recognized the weak, quavering voice instantly. We exchanged a few pleasantries and then he asked me, "Is the Lamm farm still for sale?" I told him about the option and how we were trying to raise the money. He knew about the farm after reading the excellent photo story that Olga Carlile had run in The Journal-Standard that explained our plight. Harry then said, "I've been looking for a suitable memorial for my wife and daughter. I think I'll just and daughter. I think I'll just buy it for them." "The whole thing?" I asked in amazement. "Yes, the whole thing. It'll take me a couple of weeks to raise the money," he said.

We had a committee meeting scheduled for the next day at the downtown office. We had printed up envelopes, pledge cards, and bulletins. I posted a note on the door, "MEETING CANCELED DUE TO GOOD NEWS!" It all came true as Harry had promised. We eventually built a first class footbridge over Crane's Creek, established a nine acre tall prairie grass reserve and an additional two acres of savanna prairie. Our treasury grew to over $50,000, which we would need. Oakdale Park was now approaching one hundred acres in size.

The Benny Brown farm, owned by his mother's estate, encompassed the thirty-nine acres just to the west of the original church camp across Crane's Grove Road. Mr. Woody Burt, the attorney for the estate, realized that he had a conflict of interest, as a past president of the foundation, though he thought this would make an excellent addition to Oakdale. He opted to have a public auction for the sale of the land.

I arranged for a line of credit of $200,000 with the First National Bank. I hoped we wouldn't need all of it. I then called a special Trustees meeting to present the opportunity we had before us. I asked for the authority to represent the foundation at the auction with the hope of being the winning bidder. I offered to purchase the first acre at the final price. Our interest was only in the south thirty four acres, which included the creek bottom of beautiful timber land.

The auction started out as usual with the curious bidders dropping out early. Three serious bidders gradually kept bumping up the price. A Chicago area developer, a local developer and I were still in the game. The bid stood at $157,000. I took a deep breath and offered $160,000. "Sold!" the auctioneer finally exclaimed. We may have paid a high price at $4800 per square acre but in the end it was worth it. We now needed to come up with the money.

There is an established truth in fund-raising. It is always full of surprises. Our most pleasant surprise came from the children of Jean Smith (Mrs. Edgar) Newell. We had appealed to them for help, as their mother, Jean, had donated $40,000 toward a previous effort. Her son, Allan, said that they had agreed to sponsor ten acres at a price of $48,000. The newest acquisition was named "Jean Smith Newell Memorial Parkland" in their mother's honor.

Today, the foundation is solvent with a net worth of almost one-half million dollars. We are in a position to continue supporting our parks. A recent effort of the foundation was to lend its name to the fund-raising efforts of Kids Kastle in Krape Park. We hope to continue developing our park system in order that future generations can appreciate the natural beauty of the area. Many wonderful people have made all of this possible. I was honored and privileged to have done my part.

Thomas Ennenga

Always bear in mind that your own resolution to success is more important than any other one thing.

Abraham Lincoln

How Kellog's Grove Got Recognized as a National Monument or Historical Site

It took a lot to convince everyone that the Kellog's Grove site should be a national monument. After all, it *was* the site of the killing of 23 militia men (whom Abraham Lincoln helped to bury) and it was one of the main roads for the lead wagons going to the Peoria smelters. Jim Thorpe, as well as a distant relative of Black Hawk, were here to dedicate it. We are quite proud of the work put forth to its recognition as an historical site.

We had a big supper in the firehouse at Kent with our Native American friends from Oklahoma. Before the celebration, a beautiful cloud formation in the sky above the Grove was seen and the Native Americans were able to read the signs in the clouds. This was highly favorable for both sides.

I sat beside a great niece of Black Hawk, a very interesting woman who carried on a very good conversation with me. She was glad to meet our committee, and she gave me her business card. (I had to look it up, sometimes these names get confusing.) Sherman Virtue gave a brief talk on the Indian War at Kellog's Grove where the militia tried to trap the Indians, but got trapped themselves. Abe Lincoln and his crew were waylaid in Oakdale Campgrounds and didn't get there until the following day, just in time to bury the dead. Apparently the Indians took care of their own because none were buried at Kellog's Grove.

Jim Thorpe, War Secretary for Indian Affairs in Washington, explained the purpose of the Department of Indian Affairs and their efforts to help relations between the races. After speeches by Sherman Virtue and Roger Hill, we had an Indian War Dance by the Uray Dancers, a scout troop from Freeport, and a display by the Black Powder Boys, a group of mountain men who came in and exhibited how they lived in Black Hawk's days. This was a very interesting day thanks to Mr. Virtue and his committee and the Kent Fire Department who have always kept the grounds mowed and in fine shape. Mr. Strohacker from Pearl City displayed his collection of Indian artifacts. About 1,000 people attended this very worthwhile affair.

An old log cabin in the county, donated to the park, was moved to the Grove by a few men and a large truck for permanent placement near a plaque commemorating the battle and the history of the monument given to us by the government and mounted on a granite stone. Sherman Virtue who lives just west of the monument and has a winter home in Branson, Missouri, is a very happy man.

Go out to the Kellog Grove Monument and take advantage of the work that's been done; the Kent Fire Department keeps the grass mowed and the pump primed, so have a picnic or take a walk. The following people are responsible for getting the site classified as a National Monument: Sherman Virtue of Kent; Mr. Krupke of Lena; and Evelyn Dameier, Roger Hill and Rev. Whitney from Pearl City. We had a real working committee, and we all are proud of our accomplishment. There is so much history in this area. All you have to do is start digging and someone has an old artifact or kinfolk who helped develop this area.

(I am sorry if I missed any of the people that helped in this effort.)

Roger Hill

Thanks to art, instead of seeing one world, our own, we see it multiplied and as many original artists as there are, so many worlds are at our disposal.

Marcel Proust

The Freeport Art Museum/ Cultural Center:
Its Establishment and Move to North Harlem Avenue

When the W.T. Rawleigh Company was in its final struggle for survival it appeared very likely that the collection of art acquired by W.T. Rawleigh might leave the city. It had been housed on company property here for many years.

John Doak, a prominent Freeport citizen and the J.C. Penney store manager for many years, had an interest in cultural matters and viewed this prospect with dismay. He gathered around him others with a similar bent and set out to keep the extensive Rawleigh collection in Freeport as the foundation for an art museum. Notable among these were Arde (Mrs. Woodruff) Burt, William Koenig, JoAnne Schulz, my wife, Ida Lou Ennenga and others.

After the Rawleigh Company agreed to give the collection to the Art Museum should they be able to acquire a site, the Board of Education was asked to sell the vacant Henney School in the Third Ward to them for one dollar. They agreed and things proceeded.

Five years later, the Museum Board decided on a more accessible and attractive location. The recently vacated Harlem School building was available. My wife, Ida Lou, was President of the Museum and made this move her prime objective. She had always served as my friend and counselor on all prior efforts so I agreed to help with this one. Many knowledgeable people predicted failure.

$250,000 was needed to adapt the Harlem School and pay for the move. Woody Burt also put his shoulder to the wheel to help make it happen. We tapped the expertise and contacts of a wide group of friends. This was like no other effort in my experience.

We sold endorsements of galleries and areas to companies and to individuals. In the end we succeeded and the Freeport Art Museum and Cultural Center continues as a unique asset in our community.

Thomas Ennenga

I have a dream that my four little children will one day live in a nation where they will not be judged by the color of their skin but by the content of their character.

Martin Luther King, Jr.

King Community Campus

In a city that has always shown its concern and compassion for their fellow citizens, Freeport once again perhaps displayed its greatest act of community spirit. On a spring day in May of 1994 more than 300 key community leaders gathered to kickoff the "Unite a Community - Build a Dream" fund-raiser for a new Martin L. King, Jr. Community Services of Illinois facility. The Mayor, aldermen, business leaders, community leaders and ordinary citizens were present to launch this 3.5 million-dollar campaign. During the ensuing months, the campaign grew from just a few people involved to encompass individuals from throughout the country. In August, 1994, there was a great ground breaking ceremony which was a part of a larger city-wide celebration of the Lincoln Douglas Debate ceremony. Yes, the community was celebrating a great moment from the past, as well as for the future.

On November 19, 1995, the new King Community Campus opened its doors to more than 1,000 children and families needing their services. The facility houses four distinct organizations, Martin Luther King, Jr. Community Services Inc. and its sister division, Boys and Girls Club of Freeport. Also, the Amity Day Care Center and the Northwestern Illinois Community Action Agency's Headstart Program. Here within this 45,000 square foot facility services for children from 0-18 were available, a first of its kind in Freeport and Illinois.

This was a monumental occasion for our city, but let me provide a little background on how it all started. It was a hot summer day in 1993. After working one of our usual Saturdays, Rev. Charles Collins, CEO of MLKCSI and myself were taking a ride around the city. We happened to ride past Mr. Ramon Alvarez's(V.P. of Honeywell MICRO SWITCH) house and noticed him working in the yard. We stopped to say hello and began talking to him about an idea we were contemplating about building a new facility. During our discussion, Mr. Alvarez's neighbor, Mr. Dan Heine, CEO of Mercantile Bank, noticed us and came over. We also included him in our idea of a new facility. These two men thought there was some merit to the idea and decided a meeting should be convened to discuss it in more detail.

Several weeks later, a meeting was convened in the board room of Mercantile Bank. In attendance were the four of us from the first meeting and Mayor Dick Weis. The discussion was candid. After much discussion, we decided to continue to meet to pursue the possibility. Several meetings later, it was brought to the attention of another agency which was in need of a facility and would like to join the discussions. It was agreed and Amity Day Care entered the talks for a possible new facility. MLKCSI board members met with Amity Day Care Center board members to "iron out" what the possibilities could be. During these meetings, another agency brought its concerns of needing permanent space and the parties involved agreed to allow them to join, thus Head Start became a partner and their board members joined the discussion. The group brought different key individuals within the community to discuss the process and its possibilities. They cordially named themselves Project Collaboration(P.C.).

It was agreed by all agencies that if a fundraising campaign was going to be done, it needed to include all facets of the community. Everyone should be able to afford to give to this community endeavor. A method was identified as to incorporate all parts of the community and all the parties agreed that Project Collaboration(P.C.) would proceed forward. P.C. worked on its mission, purpose, and goal. They identified other key people who could be involved in the success of this fund-raiser. The group agreed to the campaign logo of "Unite a Community - Build a Dream." This directly benefits what their mission statement and purpose to..." help prepare children in our community for success in life by cooperating to assure that individual agency resources, energies, skills, and commitment are efficiently, systematically, and synergistically coordinated to meet this ultimate goal: THAT ALL CHILDREN IN OUR COMMUNITY WILL GROW UP IN A STRONG, HEALTHY FAMILY AND COMMUNITY ENVIRONMENT MEETING THEIR POTENTIAL AND BELIEVING IN THEMSELVES."

Project Collaboration believed it needed an experienced well-known person to lead the campaign and looked to Mr. Jack Myers (former successful businessman) to be that person. Mr. Myers agreed and gathered the best community citizens to assist him in making the goal. He rallied his cadre as much as possible. He was clearly the right person for the job. He met weekly with the leaders of each of the campaign areas, as well as met individually with representatives of the four agencies. He kept a running tally of how much money was needed to be raised daily, weekly, monthly in order for the campaign to be a success. Mr. Myers said in order for this campaign to be a success, everyone involved had to believe in their agency. He became intimately involved in each agency's goals for their clientele.

As agency representatives, we made it a must to talk to every possible civic group, major gathering or church function throughout the city of Freeport. The local media was cooperative in every way to the campaign. Many citizens were recruited for their own personal ability. P.C. began to see its role become more than just the building of King Community Campus, but to look at the way human services are providing programs to the citizens of the community. The members of P.C. made a commitment to continue the group after the campaign.

One spring day in May 1994, Project Collaboration took its campaign to the public. The "Unite a Community - Build a Dream" became part of every household, church and school. There were T-shirts, buttons, cards, posters, bricks, cups, etc. to get the message out. Well you know the rest of the story. The building is completed, more than 1,000 children are now using the facility on a monthly basis.

As I walk down the hallways of this wonderful building every day, I think about all the hard work that went into its creation. I ponder about all the people who came together as a true community to make this happen. I dream about the impact it will have on the youth who come through these doors daily. I feel with confidence they will benefit from it and the citizens will be quite happy that in 1994 they came together to "Unite a Community and Build a Dream."

Tracy Johnson
President of Martin L. King Jr. Community Services of Illinois

Steve Snyder

The true object of all human life is play. Earth is a task garden; heaven is a playground.

G.K. Chesterton

Kids Kastle
If We Build It ,They Will Come

The major emphasis for Kiwanis International has been exemplified by the slogan, Young Children-Priority One. The Lincoln-Douglas Kiwanis Club of Freeport, Illinois, took that message to heart during May of 1992. The Kiwanis motto, "We Build," was never more evident than during those five glorious days. The final result was a 14,000 square- foot playground, Kids Kastle, completed on May 10,1992.

Our initial proposal to the Freeport Park Board was, "Give us a location and we'll give you a playground." The Robert Leathers Company was contacted. The Park Board gave us a tentative site on which to build. The project had begun in earnest.

A representative from the Leathers Company arrived for the first visit on October 23,1991. He met with exuberant groups of students in their classrooms. Each student had their own ideas of what they wanted. Circular slides, big swings, mazes, climbing towers, and sliding wires. One day and hundreds of ideas later, the first draft of the playground was presented to the community in the Freeport

High School cafeteria. The response was overwhelming. Many names were suggested, many were considered, and finally the students' suggestion of *Kids Kastle* was chosen.

The original plans had designs for a volcano maze, upside down house, mirror maze, and a tree house. We were aiming for at least twenty-five percent of the playground to be handicapped accessible. We were told that the cost of the project would be around $70,000. We had to get busy and in a hurry!

Multiple fundraisers were put together by Friends of the Kastle. Our Lincoln-Douglas Kiwanis had committed ten thousand dollars. Much of that was raised during our annual gala raffle in February. A concert at the Masonic Temple drew hundreds of people. Sweatshirts and tee shirts were sold. Various raffles were held. People donated part of the proceeds of their own businesses. Corporate donations from area businesses were provided. A penny drive at the Lincoln Mall saw hundreds of children line up to dump the change from their piggy banks into the giant change machine. Little children donated their allowances. Each one wanted to participate in any way they could. The outpouring of love and dedication for the project sustained the core committee during our moments of doubt that we could raise the money for our dream. A dream that became the dream of a community.

The design was laid out the evening of Tuesday, May 5. The money had been raised, and the architects were encouraged by the incredible organization and arrangements that the committee chairpersons were responsible for. The anticipation hung heavy in the air. There was no time left for doubt. It was a time for single-minded action and coordinated effort. Wednesday morning at seven a.m. almost three hundred men and women waited as if at the start of a race. Let's get to work. The foremen had all been prepared and waited for their teams. The sun rose with a special fluorescence to greet the day. The next five days were a gift from the heavens-sunny, clear, and in the seventies. Short sleeves and shorts were the general attire for the week. The sweat and joy of the workers mixed as they toiled in the glorious day's task.

The next morning all the telephone poles had been lifted and secured into their respective holes. Each new group of eager workers was taken to one of the architects who briefed them before sending them to a foreman. Each group of volunteers was assigned to the prefabrication area where everything was built , sanded, or finished or to the construction area where everything from prefab was fastened or cemented. The drone of the routers hummed along throughout the day making sure that no rough edges would be on the wood. There was tremendous pride in each worker's job. Each person wanted to let their child, grandchild or neighbor know the area that he or she had worked on.

The next three days saw *Kids Kastle* take on a life of its own. The spires were lifted by the boom operator to the top of the towers as most of the volunteers stopped for a moment to watch the awe-inspiring action. Our Kastle had taken hold of Freeport. The most incredible site was the mile long line up of cars and the constant flow of traffic as people and their families came to see the playground rise like a phoenix from the ground. It reminded me of the final scene in the movie, "Field of Dreams", as the cars continued into the early hours of dusk and the last of the diehards continued, wanting to finish "just one last piece." Our raffle theme, "If we build it, they will come," turned out to be prophetic.

The children and their parents and grandparents began to gather around the periphery of their playground around four p.m. on Sunday, May tenth, Mother's Day. The sound of a few drills and manual sanding continued as we inspected the site for the final time. Gary Quinn of *The Journal Standard* spoke of community pride and about what we can do when we work as one. The organizing committee brought forth several of the children and in a touching ceremony handed over the deed to Rick Pyle, Superintendent of the Park District. He lead the children in a ribbon cutting ceremony and at six-thirty p.m. the children swarmed onto their *Kids Kastle* from the four corners of the park.

As I stood on the edge of the playground holding my wife, Irena's, hand, I felt the pride of a community. I wandered onto the playground where my daughter ran up to me, hugging me, kissing me, and saying, "Thank you, daddy! Thank you for Kids Kastle!" I felt the pride of fatherhood. I realized that we share with one another through our actions, words, and deeds. We often lead our lives quietly and think that there isn't much that we can do to change things. I realized that we leave a legacy by what we give, by what we share, and by what we dream. The hours of preparation and construction, the thousands of volunteers brought together, the over eighty thousand dollars raised for a project valued at over two hundred and fifty thousand dollars were all a small price to pay for the gleeful expressions on the children's faces and the squeals of delight from their hearts.

The sun was setting on this unforgettable day. Tomorrow we would go back to the "real world" of our regular jobs, and the children would return to school. I realized that the dream Steve Spyrison, and I had, and Cindy Fishburn and the organizing committee had labored for, was not just an inspiration to me about working together for Young Children: Priority One. It was a lesson in community spirit and community pride. Everyone put aside their egos and prejudices for five incredible days when we shared our time, talents, and energy for the love of our children, grandchildren, and children not yet born. We came together in Krape Park to build for the love of community.

Roland Tolliver

Concluding Thoughts

Thank you for your part in reading or sharing these stories. We feel that the stories touch on what we believe to be the core principles of life. On this journey our challenges are to nourish and develop our body-mind-spirit, our "SELF" which allows us to fulfill our purpose, our mission: to share and care with others.

Perhaps the greatest gift we can give our children and each other is to live and exemplify the basic values:

HONESTY
AWARENESS
RESPONSIBILITY

As we continue on our journey, seek to be the grandest vision of yourself.

It has been our honor to be a part of this creation.

Thank you.

The Authors

About the Author

Roland A. Tolliver, D.P.M. is a practicing, board certified podiatrist in Freeport, Illinois. He and his family moved to Northwest Illinois in 1990 in search of a community in which to raise their family and to be able to contribute to their community. Dr. Tolliver has found the community to be more enriching than he ever imagined.

He has been a member of the Lincoln-Douglas Kiwanis Club of Freeport since 1990, having served in various leadership roles. He was awarded the Distinguished President award for his service as club president from 1994-1995. He has been elected to serve as his division's Lieutenant Governor for the years 1999-2000. Roland graduated from the Highland Community College Leadership Institute in 1997. Dr. Tolliver is a frequent lecturer within the community for various organizations, including the Arthritis Foundation, Freeport Memorial Hospital's Top 50 program, and for Kiwanis.

Dr. Tolliver has spent the past five years working toward developing his leadership skills for his professional, community and church roles. He is a graduate of Mastery University with Anthony Robbins. He has also attended various workshops on speaking and writing, as well as personal development, most notably he participated with Mark Victor Hansen and Jack Canfield at their seminar in Long Beach, California. He is a member of the National Speakers Association.

Dr. Tolliver and Dr. Spyrison contributed their time, energy and motivation as the originators and coordinators, along with Cindy Fishburn, on the development and construction of Kids Kastle in Krape Park in 1991-1992.

Dr. Tolliver and his wife, Irena, live in Freeport with their daughters, Mary, Veronica, Claire, and Teresa.

He wrote in his podiatry school yearbook that he wanted to live in a rural community where he could contribute something back to the people who allow him to practice podiatric medicine. Dr. Tolliver appears to be fulfilling his wish and he feels privileged to be a part of such a wonderful community.

You can contact Dr. Tolliver at:

Freeport Podiatry Services
1815 West Church Street
Freeport, Illinois 61032
Tel(815)232-8015 of Fax(815)235-1376
Email: frptpod@mwci.net

About the Author

Stephen Spyrison, D.D.S. is a practicing dentist in Freeport, Illinois. He moved to Northwest Illinois in 1980 to establish his private practice. He met his wife, Vicki, here and has become an integral part of the community.

Steve has been a member of the Lincoln-Douglas Kiwanis Club of Freeport since 1980. He has served as chairman of various committees, as a board member, and served as president from 1992-1993. Steve is a 1997 graduate of Leadership Institute of Highland Community College. Dr. Spyrison is actively involved in the U.S. Grant Dental Society, is a past president, and lectures on dental care.

Dr. Spyrison has served on many organizations throughout the area. He is currently the chairman for Northwest Illinois Trail Association/Jane Addams Trail and a member of the Stephenson County Health Department. He is a past vice-president of the YMCA of Northwest Illinois Board of Directors, former member of Stephenson County Crimestop, and past president of the Freeport Choral Society.

Dr. Spyrison presented the original idea for a community playground. He and Dr. Tolliver were the co-developers and subsequently coordinators, along with Cindy Fishburn, on the Kids Kastle project in Krape Park from 1991-1992.

Dr. Spyrison and his wife, Vicki, live in Freeport with their two sons, Ben and Tyler. Sarah, their daughter, is a sophomore at Wittenberg University in Ohio.

Dr. Spyrison has established himself as an active member of the community, who is a leader by example. He has dedicated himself to helping worthwhile causes in Freeport and Northwest Illinois.

You can contact Dr. Spyrison at:

Stephen Spyrison, D.D.S.
624 Terra West
Freeport, Illinois 61032
Tel(815)232-7012 or Fax(815)233-4316

Kastle Publishing

We hope you enjoyed this book. If you would like to order additional copies, please send $15.00 plus $3.00 per book for shipping and handling to:

Kastle Publishing
Dr. Roland Tolliver
1815 W. Church Street
Freeport, Illinois 61032
Fax 815.235.1376

Please make checks payable to Lincoln-Douglas Kiwanis.

Childhood Memories

The first three stanzas of **On Thanksgiving Day** on page 40 were inadvertently omitted from the printing of this book. We regret the error. As a courtesy to the author and readers we have included the complete text as submitted by the author, *Vera Emmert Johansen.*

Roland & Steve

On Thanksgiving Day

We thank God for our homes, for health,
For food and friends so dear,
But I prefer Thanksgiving Day
Each day throughout the year.

I'm thankful for a baby's smile,
For children at their play,
For spiders spinning out their webs,
For breath of new-mown hay.

I'm thankful for the golden grain
That ripples in the breeze,
For water cool, for song of birds,
That nest among the trees.

I'm thankful for the distant hum
Of trucks and motor cars,
For honking geese, for blizzard winds
For twinkling of the stars.

I'm thankful for the voice of rain
Upon the thirsty earth,
Such blessings, although common-place
Are blessings of great worth.

They bring a joy and inner peace
That linger in my soul.
To God I offer thanks **each day**
For these have made me whole.

Vera Emmert Johansen